Death Ship of Halifax Harbour

Steven Laffoley

Pottersfield Press, Lawrencetown Beach, Nova Scotia, Canada

Library and Archives Canada Cataloguing in Publication

Laffoley, Steven Edwin

    Death ship of Halifax Harbour / Steven Laffoley.

ISBN 978-1-897426-09-8

1. Halifax (N.S.)--History--19th century.
2. McNabs Island (N.S.)--History--19th century.
3. Cholera--Nova Scotia--History--19th century.
4. Immigrants--Diseases--Nova Scotia--History--19th century.
5. Ships--Nova Scotia--History--19th century. I. Title.

FC2345.M32L33 2009   971.6'22502   C2009-902697-X

Cover design by Gail LeBlanc

Pottersfield Press acknowledges the financial support of the Government of Canada through the Book Publishing Industry Development Program for our publishing activities. We also acknowledge the ongoing support of the Canada Council for the Arts, which last year invested $20.1 million in writing and publishing throughout Canada. We also thank the Province of Nova Scotia for its support through the Department of Tourism, Culture and Heritage.

Pottersfield Press
83 Leslie Road
East Lawrencetown, Nova Scotia, Canada, B2Z 1P8
Website: www.pottersfieldpress.com
To order, phone toll-free 1-800-NIMBUS9 (1-800-646-2879)
Printed in Canada

For Dick Twomey
Teacher, Mentor and Friend

Acknowledgements

My deep appreciation to the following for their help in bringing this book together: Lesley Choyce, Julia Swan, Peggy Amirault and Gail LeBlanc for their wisdom, enthusiasm and skill; David Wiggin and Deborah Goodfellow for their advice, assistance and encouragement; and, of course, Bernice and Emma for their unqualified support.

Contents

"'Tis the best use of Fate to teach a fatal courage. Go face the fire at sea or the cholera in your friend's home, or the burglar in your own, or what danger lies in the way of duty, knowing you are guarded by the cherubim of Destiny. If you believe in Fate to your harm, believe it, at least, for your good. For, if Fate is so prevailing, man also is part of it, and can confront fate with fate. If the Universe have these savage accidents, our atoms are as savage in resistance."

– Ralph Waldo Emerson, Concord, 1860

Preface

*F*ate is weird – really.

Consider these words from our oldest English tale, the Anglo-Saxon epic poem *Beowulf*: *"Gaeo a wyrd swa hio scel."* In rough translation, this modest word-horde means, "Fate goes as fate must." Which is to say, "wyrd" is fate.

And fate is weird.

Mind you, for the marauding, mead-soaked Anglo-Saxons who lived their lives in pastoral England a thousand years ago, the word wyrd meant something altogether different than the "uncanny" or "bizarre" we ascribe to it today. Back then, amid the timber houses, grazing sheep, and bearded farmers named Cuthred and Egbert, the word wyrd meant a deep belief in the weaving interconnectedness of all human thoughts and actions. Wyrd shaped the past, and wyrd would shape the future.

Yet, paradoxically, for Cuthred and Egbert and all the Anglo-Saxons, wyrd also allowed each person to live a life in brave defiance of fate. It allowed each person to craft an individual destiny, to weave some part of a thread through the interconnected strands of wyrd's great tapestry. This was the story of Beowulf: one man's defiant rebuke of, and final acceptance of, inexorable fate.

Which is wyrd.

The tale that follows is also wyrd. Certainly, it begins weirdly enough, with me standing at the edge of an old wharf in Eastern Passage, Nova Scotia, trying to hold down my breakfast.

Why was I standing at an old wharf, wrestling down my gorge?

Well, I was there in search of a "death ship." Or at least I was there in search of the fragmented historical whispers of a death ship, an elegant old steamer that limped into the darkness of Halifax Harbour during the early hours of April 9, 1866, with more than a thousand Irish and German emigrants squeezed into its cramped, creaking hold. And I was in search of what travelled with them and, in fact, inside many of them: the cholera of the fourth great cholera epidemic – an epidemic that laid waste to hundreds of cities, towns, and villages, killing tens of thousands from Mecca to Manhattan. And finally, in that rich Anglo-Saxon sense of the word wyrd, I was in search of the narrative threads that somehow wove this tapestry-tale together.

My search for this death ship began some months earlier, on a warm summer's day, when I was visiting the Nova Scotia Archives, casually trolling the microfiche shelves for serendipitous bits of stories. Having set myself up at a corner projection machine, I spooled my way through files of historical jetsam, until I happened upon a twenty-year-old medical journal containing a number of articles devoted to the sawdust-dry subject of infectious diseases and local quarantines. Such a source was not the normal reserve of compelling tales, but tucked away on page six was a brief account of a cholera ship in Halifax Harbour. And though the article was singularly focused on the quarantine efforts of Nova Scotia Premier Dr. Charles Tupper and Health Officer for the Port of Halifax Dr. John Slayter, I found myself reading between the lines, imagining the nameless German and Irish emigrants who came face to face with fear and fate in the close quarters of the cholera ship's hold.

My curiosity was piqued.

So, as time allowed over the next few months, I rummaged through more spools of archival microfiche and waves of archival Internet sites. I thumbed through old tattered books and still older frayed maps. I perused myriad pictures and amateur paintings. And slowly, thread by thread, my tapestry-tale began to take shape.

I was pleasantly reacquainted with famous faces of old Halifax – Dr. Charles Tupper, Joseph Howe, and Dr. John Slayter among others, about whom I had written before in *Hunting Halifax: In Searh of History, Mystery and Murder*. And I was introduced to new faces, the common folk of this story – among them a German labourer, an Iranian bricklayer, an English pastor, an Irish revolutionary, and an American missionary – all of whose lives were vibrant threads in the tapestry, all inexorably intersecting, in one way or another, on an island in the mouth of Halifax Harbour. In fact, the more I explored this tale, the more I was compelled by the tangential and fateful interwoven threads of these human narratives. Frankly, it was wyrd. Each time I pulled at a local thread, a distant one in the tapestry would unravel. And each time I tugged at a distant thread, the local corner of the tapestry would pull.

Admittedly, this deep interconnectedness left me struggling to find the singular, compelling theme of my tale – until I found a curious letter written by a Dr. Cyrus Hamlin. Cyrus Hamlin was born in the small town of Waterford, Maine, in 1811. A precocious child, he grew to be a young man of unusual ambition and moral stature. When he was old enough, he entered Bowdwin College, in Brunswick, Maine, and then attended Bangor Theological Seminary. Graduating in 1837, he felt the call of service – and perhaps the lure of adventure – and left Maine in 1838, travelling to Constantinople (now Istanbul), Turkey, where he served first as a missionary and then founded a boys' school for the minority Armenians.

As fate would have it, Hamlin was working at this boys' school when the Crimean War began in 1853. The conflict forced many families to leave the city and, as a consequence, the school closed. Without work, Hamlin turned to his skill as a cook and opened a bakery. By happenstance, not long afterward, a British officer watched a load of Hamlin's bread being ferried across the Bosphorus River, and he promptly offered Hamlin a sizable military contract to supply the British Army with baked goods. Naturally, Hamlin agreed. By the time the war ended in 1856, Hamlin found himself in possession of a princely £25,000 with which he returned to education, founding Robert College in 1863, a school that remains the oldest operating American school outside of America.

It was while working at Robert College in the summer of 1865 that Hamlin witnessed the fourth great cholera epidemic, which had travelled with hajj pilgrims from Mecca to Constantinople, and from Constantinople to Europe and beyond. As the epidemic spread, Hamlin waded hip-deep into this cholera crisis and provided aid and comfort throughout the city wherever he could. Through the long summer and late fall, he fought the disease as it raged unabated, until the chill air of winter brought the epidemic to an end.

It was when cholera was finally in retreat that Hamlin – recognizing that the illness would surely make its way to North America – decided to compose a letter to family and friends, informing them about the disease and offering them the wisdom he had learned from fighting it. And so, in early winter, he took up his pen and wrote a lengthy description of cholera, its causes, and its cures. He then mailed it to his family in Waterville, Maine.

In Maine, the letter was well-received. Shortly after its arrival, it was published in the local paper. Then it was published again in other papers along the east coast. And, finally, as the cholera epidemic reached the shores of North America in the spring of 1866, the letter was printed in *The New York*

Times, after which Hamlin's "scientific" medical advice became omnipresent, and Hamlin himself became famous.

Some years later, when Hamlin retired from teaching and returned to Maine, he wrote about this famous letter in his memoir, *Among the Turks*. "No quarantine has been found effectual to stop the progress of cholera," he wrote in the book. "It comes irregularly every five to ten years, seeks out its victims, does its work ruthlessly, and departs. Its most terrible ravages were in the onset of 1865. During the last days of August of that year, business ceased and the great capital attended to nothing but the burial of the dead. By the actual count of an English friend, more bodies were carried out of one gate than the whole number of deaths reported by government; the latter hoping to diminish the panic by false reports. On one of those days I went to three pharmacies in search of a new supply of laudanum, and I met but fourteen persons, although I passed through streets where one is always jostled by the crowd. I met near the bridge that crosses the Golden Horn, on the Constantinople side, an Armenian friend who said, 'Don't come this way, I have been trying to dodge the dead and can't do it.'

"On the first day of September there was an evident diminution in the number of new cases, and in the virulence of the attacks. Its force was spent. Every day lifted up the gloom from the city and had not a terrible conflagration made many thousands homeless, there would have been a burst of joy. The fire swept from the Golden Horn to the Sea of Marmora, chiefly through Mussulman quarters, and nothing could withstand the fury of its course. At the close of these calamities I wrote the following letter home. It was widely published at the time and, as it contains the results of much experience, it may be worth preserving."

For me, reading this description more than a hundred years later, Hamlin's words possessed a strange, paradoxical confidence: "it may be worth preserving." This personal confidence seemed to capture the hubristic confidence of the age, an age steeped in meticulous "objective" science and an inevitable march of human progress. And yet, with a hundred years of hindsight, nearly all of Hamlin's "science-based" advice was simply – and often deadly – wrong. What Hamlin offered in his letter to his "friends back home," and to so many in North America, was little more than a shaman's dance for the dying and the dead.

Still, insofar as my tale of a death ship in Halifax Harbour was concerned, Hamlin's cholera letter offered a deep, though unintentional, truth – a thematic thread that wove itself through the whole of my tale. In his letter, I glimpsed a deep-rooted connection between two ages – a mid-nineteenth century broadly obsessed with daily newspaper reports of imminent threats: of deadly diseases and radical revolutionaries, leading to a perpetually fearful populous placing their faith in false prophets and false prophecies; and an early twenty-first century broadly obsessed with around the clock cable news reports of imminent threats: of cold-hearted terrorists and calamitous tsunamis, leading to a perpetually fearful populous placing their faith in false prophets and false prophecies. Naturally, I wondered: did this past somehow, inexorably, shape our present?

Or was that just wyrd?

Such questions compelled me to follow the story threads, wherever they wove, including to the edge of an old wharf in Eastern Passage, Nova Scotia, where I found myself staring queasily into the dark, choppy waters of the Atlantic Ocean in search of some physical evidence of a death ship in Halifax Harbour.

What follows is what I found.

*   *   *

One final thought: to the degree that fragmentary evidence, contradictory memory, and historical black holes make such things possible, everything in this tale – the events described, the details discussed, and the words attributed – are all accurate, or at least all reasonably accurate. That said, from time to time, to keep the narrative flame burning, I blew across some faint embers.

Such is the way of wyrd.

Indeed, in reflecting on how this particular word-horde took shape, I was reminded of a line from another Anglo-Saxon tale, "The Riming Poem," which goes like this: *"Me paet wyrd gewaef"* – "Wyrd wove this for me."

And so it did.

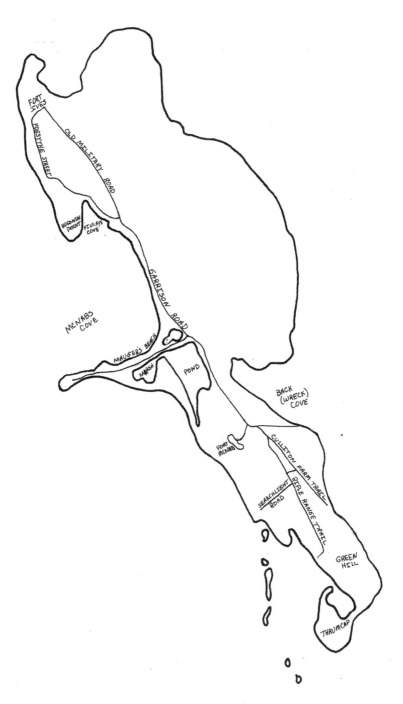

McNab's Island

1

The Cholera

"The cholera, which has just left us after committing fearful ravages is making its way into Europe, and will probably cross the Atlantic before another Summer has passed. Having been providentially compelled to have a good degree of practical acquaintance with it, and to see it in all its forms and stages during each of its invasions of Constantinople, I wish to make my friends … some suggestions, which may relieve anxiety, or be of practical use.

"On the approach of the cholera every family member should be prepared to treat it without waiting for a physician. It does its work so expeditiously, that while you are waiting for the doctor it is done. If you prepare for it, it will not come. I think there is no disease, which may be avoided with so much certainty as the cholera. But providential circumstances, of the thoughtless indiscretions of some member of a household, may invite the attack, and the challenge will never be refused. It will probably be made in the night, [while] your physician has been

called in another direction and you must treat the case yourself
or it will be fatal."
                    – Dr. Cyrus Hamlin, Constantinople, 1865

Not so long ago, on an uncomfortably muggy morning in
early autumn, I found myself standing listlessly at the
end of a wide, battered wharf, in Eastern Passage, Nova Scotia,
breathing in a thick miasma of rotted fish and diesel fuel.
Above me, a flock of agitated seagulls circled and shrieked,
keenly eyeing two rows of ramshackle fishing boats moored
to either side of the wharf. Behind me, six fishermen in ball
caps, jeans, and t-shirts stood in a loose semi-circle, talking
shop, drinking coffee, and smoking cigarettes. As I watched the
gulls and listened to the fishermen, I took in a deep breath –
and quickly wished I hadn't. The cigarette smoke had mixed
liberally with the rotted fish and diesel fuel, and my stomach
lurched. Involuntarily, I turned to my right and leaned over the
wharf's edge, hoping to keep breakfast where I had put it. And
for a moment, I wondered why I hadn't stayed in bed.

Of course, I knew the answer. I had come to this wharf's
edge in Eastern Passage, to a place called Fisherman's Cove –
a mostly faux tourist village of trinket shops and fast-food joints
– to follow my Muse. And of all the things one might muse
about, on an uncomfortably muggy morning in early autumn, I
chose to muse about this: why do we fear blue mists?

Let me explain.

I arrived at Fisherman's Cove by car about half an hour
earlier, lazily crossing the Macdonald Bridge from Halifax and
meandering south along a winding road through Dartmouth
and Eastern Passage under mostly overcast skies with hints of
blue and the vaguest promise of sun. When I turned into Fisherman's Cove – which, in truth, was little more than a road-
side pullover – I found myself in a large gravelled parking lot,

where three lonely cars suggested the near passing of the tourist season. Reaching into the backseat, I gathered my things into a small blue rucksack and left the car, walking slowly along a pine boardwalk, past a long row of similarly shaped tourist huts to number twenty-four: a small, one-room information centre painted blue.

Inside the hut, I was greeted by a dizzying display of colourful brochures and illustrated maps that nearly filled the walls, while similarly adorned wooden cases sat willy-nilly on the linoleum floor. I strolled casually among the offerings, spending time perusing the maps and pocketing the odd brochure promoting exciting adventures and exotic locations in clipped sentences and glowing testimonials, but soon enough found myself overwhelmed. So I approached the desk where two sullen, tartan-wearing tourist attendants engaged in sharp-tongued conversation about someone's divorce.

"Excuse me," I gently interrupted. "Would you mind telling me how I could find the ferry to McNab's Island?"

One attendant, an older woman with a fleshy face and short hair, reluctantly stopped talking. She turned to me and sighed. "You'll want Captain Red Beard," she said. "You can't miss him. He's usually hanging out somewhere along the far end of the dock – that way." She pointed over my shoulder, wagging a thick finger at the far wall as though the dock were plainly in sight.

"Right," I said. "The far dock."

"Yes," she said. "He'll be the one wearing knee-high white rubber boots and a big red and grey beard."

"Oh," I quipped, "so that's what Santa does in the off-season."

But the attendant coolly ignored my comment and re-entered her conversation with the sullen tartan mate. With no one left to appreciate my wit, I left tourist hut twenty-four and started toward the far dock, where it was my aim to have Captain Red Beard ferry me to the shore of a largely deserted island, overgrown with thick underbrush and forest, which sits in the mouth of Halifax Harbour. There I planned to spend the day alone, searching for tangible story fragments of a death ship that once sailed into Halifax Harbour with more than a thousand immigrants from Germany and Ireland, many of whom perished horribly in one of the worst global epidemics of cholera in history.

This was how I found myself leaning over the edge of a wharf in Fisherman's Cove, on an uncomfortably muggy morning in early autumn, searching for a man in knee-high, white rubber boots answering to the name of Captain Red Beard and hoping to keep my breakfast down.

It wasn't a promising start.

As my stomach slowly settled, one of the fishing boats behind me revved its engine, sending a thick plume of blue-white smoke floating over the water. For a time, I watched the cloud of smoke shift and drift and then dissipate. As it evaporated from view, I began thinking – in a strangely tangential way – about an obscure British scientist named James Glaisher and the similar blue-white cloud he saw on the morning of July 30, 1866.

On that morning, under a mostly cloudless sky, James Glaisher strolled confidently along a groomed path that wound its way up a gentle rise to the door of an ornate, two-storey, red-brick building. Fitted with tall, white-framed windows and two squared turrets, the building was designed by Christopher Wren in 1675 for King Charles II as the first facility specifically built for scientific research in England. It was called Flamsteed House. Even after almost two hundred years, it was still used in 1866 for science – meteorological and atmospheric observations. And, as it so happened, it was also the place where James Glaisher worked as the Superintendent of the Meteorological Department of the Greenwich Observatory.

When Glaisher approached Flamsteed House that morning, he almost certainly looked up toward the unusual red time ball, which sat atop the right-side turret. Each day, at five minutes before one o'clock, the ball was slowly raised along a narrow metal pole, and then – at precisely 1:00 p.m. – it was dropped, so that ships' captains travelling along the Thames River could set their chronometers accordingly. And likely, that morning, Glaisher looked past the red time ball and noted the thick, arrow-shaped, iron weathervane that rested prominently atop the pole. It pointed steadily to the west.

Glaisher then entered the observatory, removed his coat and his hat, and turned to face the room. His tussled wave of grey hair and mutton-chop sideburns framed his handsome face – a strong chin, prominent cheekbones, and restless blue eyes. Glaisher had already made a name for himself in London science circles with his meticulous measurements of the weather and his seminal work on humidity. As well, he had earned fame as a pioneering balloonist, even breaking an altitude record of nearly eight thousand metres, before passing out.

In any case, on this particular morning, Glaisher gathered his notebooks and pencils, and meticulously organized his measuring instruments and tools. He then made his way to a heavy oak desk situated by a broad, double-framed window that overlooked a green field and a thick wood beyond. After sitting, he opened his leather-bound notebook and thumbed the broad white pages, until he found the appropriate spot for his entry. Finally, he took up his pen and attended to his morning's responsibilities: the studious observations of the day's weather.

Carefully, he recorded the temperature ("seventy degrees Fahrenheit, relatively cool for July") and observed the sky ("clear, with few clouds"), and even noted the breeze from the weathervane ("blowing in lazily from the west"). Likely, while jotting down these initial mundane observations, Glaisher thought the day wholly unexceptional.

Yet, after recording some additional details, he looked again through the window and out across the grassy fields to the edge of the woods. There, he noticed something distinctly out of place. "A dense blue mist apparent on all sides," he wrote excitedly in his notebook, "extended fully to the tops of the trees." Doubtless, the arrival of this "dense blue mist" caused Glaisher much alarm. After all, he had seen this atmospheric oddity before – twelve years before, when he studied this "dense blue mist" at the request of London's General Board of Health. In fact, he later presented his observations and findings to the British Parliament in a work dramatically tying "blue mist" to the recurring epidemics of cholera in England. His work was entitled *Appendix to Report of the Committee of Scientific Inquiries in Relation to the Cholera Epidemic of 1854.*

"The three epidemics [of cholera in 1832, 1849, and 1854]," he wrote in that report, "attended with a particular state of atmosphere, characterized by a prevalent mist, thin in high places, dense in low. During the height of the epidemic, in all cases, the reading of the barometer was remarkably high, and the atmosphere thick. In 1849 and in 1854, the temperature was above its average, and a total absence of rain and a stillness of the air amounting almost to calm, accompanied the progress of the disease on each occasion. In places near the river, the night temperatures were high, with small diurnal range, a dense torpid mist, and air charged with the many impurities arising from the exhalations of the river and adjoining marshes, a deficiency of electricity, and, as shown in 1854, a total absence of ozone, most probably destroyed by the decomposition of the organic matter with which the air in these situations is strongly charged ...

"The co-existence of Cholera with the coincident meteorological phenomena is, to say the least of it, remarkable. So is the stagnant atmosphere prevalent during the dint of Cholera in each of the three periods, and which would seem to be a necessary condition to the activity of the disease ... I cannot consider the birth of Cholera attributable solely to atmospheric influences; at the same time, the preceding pages have shown beyond a doubt, the activity of London's climate in accelerating the disease, thereby showing its progress to be intimately connected with meteorological influences."

This "dense blue mist," which Glaisher witnessed that morning in late July, remained among the trees of Greenwich, off and on, throughout that summer and fall. "This mist increased in intensity," he wrote, "when viewed through a telescope. Usually no mist can be seen when thus viewed. It increased in density during the fall of rain, although usually mist rises from rain." Yet, for James Glaisher, there was likely no real surprise in the return of this "dense blue mist," for at that same moment, in the streets and homes of London, there had come the return of cholera.

The London cholera epidemic of 1866 was part of the fourth great cholera epidemic of the nineteenth century, which ultimately killed more than 200,000 people worldwide from the early summer of 1865 to the late autumn of 1866. During those dark months, the disease moved relentlessly from Mecca to mainland Europe by pilgrim caravan and travelled unremittingly from England and Ireland, across the open Atlantic Ocean by immigrant steamer, to North America – even to the shores of McNab's Island in Halifax Harbour.

Still standing at the edge of the wharf at Fisherman's Cove, and still thinking about blue mists, I realized that the wind had now shifted and was blowing off the water against my face. Mercifully, the rich miasma of fish, fuel, and smoke receded, and I lifted my head to take in another deep breath of ocean air.

With the gulls still crying out and the fishermen still talking and smoking, I stared out across the narrow channel to a small island called Lawlor's, a modest stretch of land covered in thick groves of green trees and grassy clearings, and let my eyes drift over the pleasant foliage. Then I looked north, past Lawlor's Island, to the northern half of a second, larger island called McNab's. As with Lawlor's Island, McNab's Island boasted thick groves of still-green trees (white spruce, balsam fir, red maple, and birch) and wide clearings of grass (red fescue, colonial bent grass, rough goldenrod, and St. John's wort). On that unusually warm morning, from the distance of Fisherman's Wharf, the island seemed a peaceful and inviting place.

As I meditated on this vista, my thoughts were interrupted by the whine of an outboard motor. I glanced to my right and saw in the distance a blue aluminum boat, skipping across the water toward the wharf. Sitting in the aft, with a firm hand on the tiller, was a large man sporting a red beard. As I watched the boat approach, I thought once more about James Glaisher and his blue mist.

Glaisher's persistent notion that cholera was simply the product of bad or noxious air was hardly original. In fact, the idea of airborne illness had a long, complex history, dating back as far as the Middle Ages. "Between Cathay and Persia," wrote a chronicler of the black plague of 1348, "there rained a vast rain of fire falling in flakes like snow and burning up mountains and plains and other lands, with men and women; and then arose vast masses of smoke; and whosoever beheld this died within the space of half a day." This belief in bad air as the cause of disease was called the Miasma Theory of Illness, and its ghostly, indefinable quality made it truly terrifying.

Indeed, through 1865 and 1866, as the fourth cholera epidemic took shape, the spectral fear of miasmic illness terrified many around the world. "The New Orleans dispatches do not confirm the reports of cholera at Mobile and Key West," reported *The New York Times* on March 24, 1866. "The quarantine for Florida and coast vessels has been removed, and that for vessels from the West Indies, it is said, will soon be. This latter statement it is difficult to credit, when it is acknowledged that the disease prevails in some of the eastern Gulf Islands, though it has not reached Havana, as was once reported."

Such fears found fertile ground in the city of Halifax, too. "When," asked a local newspaper, emphatically and prophetically in early April 1866, "are the authorities going to remove those piles of cholera-inventing mud, lying on Water Street, poisoning our atmosphere and injuring the health of the neighbourhood?"

Of course, for the locals of Halifax and for many around the world, the mid-nineteenth century seemed an age positively rich with fears – local, national, and international. Throughout the spring of 1866, the local newspapers in Halifax not only beat the drums of the coming cholera, but they also heralded the threat of a Fenian invasion and the calamity of Canadian Confederation.

The Fenians were an Irish nationalist organization in the United States. In 1866, they planned, and ultimately executed, at least two invasions of Canada, with the hope of holding some portion of the country hostage to trade with the British for Irish independence. Certainly, these plans made for sensational newspaper reports. On March 17, 1866, the Halifax newspapers eagerly raised the alarm about preparations being made for the almost certain invasions.

"Yesterday evening," read one article, "the residents of the outer coves of Halifax Harbour were startled by the sudden manning of the new fortifications there by strong detachments of Artillery. These unusual demonstrations, coupled with the fact that the Boston Cunard Steamer was not met by the pilot as expected, caused great apprehension that the Fenians were coming up the Harbour at once. They had not heard the report that the steamer had been detained twenty-four hours in Boston by a heavy fog. The forts down the harbour are now thoroughly manned; and the authorities are doing all that is right and requisite under the circumstances. A rumour ran along the street to-day that a telegram from New York last night had informed our military authorities that three – some say four – Fenian gunboats had just set out from New York, but we could not trace the story to any authentic source. The Militia Force of this City will be turned out on Monday on the Common to receive arms and ammunition."

This threat would have been keenly felt in heavily Irish Halifax. Fenian fears were ripe fruit for opportunistic politicians such as Joseph Howe and Charles Tupper, both of whom proved more than willing to exploit the largely poor Irish population – caricatured for the consumption of the English Protestant population as universally sympathetic to the Fenian cause – to achieve their particular political ends, particularly with Canadian Confederation, which Nova Scotians were also made to fear.

In the early months of 1866, the existence of Nova Scotia as a member of the British Empire was under attack by those allied with Premier Charles Tupper. Tupper, against the wishes of most Nova Scotians, had already met with his counterparts in Upper and Lower Canada, and those in the other Atlantic provinces, to negotiate some form of Canadian union. An artful politician, Tupper utilized the fear of Fenian invasion to push through a vote for union in Nova Scotia. "What ever the price," noted historian Hereward Senior in his book *The Last Invasion of Canada: The Fenian Raids, 1866-1870* about the first Fenian invasion of Canada at Campobello, New Brunswick, "it was well worth it from the point of view of the Confederationist party. Sir Charles Tupper, premier of Nova Scotia, was able to get the Legislative Assembly to approve Confederation ..."

At the same time, Joseph Howe, a politician and newspaperman who passionately disagreed with union, used his formidable skills as a writer and orator to stoke fear among Nova Scotians against Confederation. Imagine what it would be like, he argued, when Nova Scotians were stripped of the British Empire's protection and forced to become citizens of a "wretched confederacy whose 'drum beat' nobody ever heard, and which has not a war ship upon the ocean, or a minister or a consul with the slightest influence abroad." Specifically,

Howe used the Fenian threat as reason to fear Confederation. "Poor old Nova Scotia," he wrote. "God help her, beset with marauders outside and enemies within, she has a hard time of it."

It was with no hint of irony that both Tupper and Howe used the Fenian threat to attract supporters to their causes. Under such an onslaught of accumulated fears, perhaps it was understandable that Haligonians and Nova Scotians were, by late March of 1866, in a constant state of worry about what terrors tomorrow might bring.

I was considering the effects of these fears when Captain Red Beard's boat pulled up alongside the battered wharf. From the water, the captain gave a quick call, and I identified myself as a would-be ferry passenger. He tossed me a line of yellow rope, which I caught and wound around a thick piece of weathered wood. When the boat was secured, the captain nimbly climbed the fixed ladder and onto the wharf. There, we briefly came to terms on travel to the island, and he invited me aboard. I cautiously climbed down the ladder and into the aluminum boat, which rocked unsteadily under my weight. I found a seat and pulled an orange life jacket over my head. While I wrestled with the life jacket's buckles, the captain climbed down the ladder, found a seat, and started up the engine. When, finally, I managed to secure the buckles of my life jacket, I turned on my aluminum bench seat and faced the water. As I did, I thought once more about the fear of cholera and Fenians and Confederation and how these individual fears seemed to fold into one another, creating a singular, almost miasmic, fear.

From the standpoint of history, such fear seemed paradoxical to me. The nineteenth century was, after all, a progressive, scientific age when irrational fear should have abated in the face of concrete science and common sense solutions. Yet

I considered that this was also an age strangely obsessed with spiritual séances and mystic clairvoyants.

In 1866, the same year as the cholera ship sailed into Halifax Harbour, famed British naturalist, geographer, and explorer Alfred Russel Wallace – the epitome of a mid-nineteenth-century science mind – wrestled with the paradox of séances in a scientific age in an essay entitled "The Scientific Aspect of the Supernatural: Indicating the desirableness of an experimental enquiry by men of science into the alleged powers of clairvoyants and mediums."

In his essay, Wallace argued, "A century ago, a telegram from 3,000 miles' distance, or a photograph taken in five seconds, would not have been believed possible, and would not have been credited on testimony, except by the ignorant and the superstitious who believed in miracles. Five centuries ago, the effects produced by the modern telescope and microscope would have been deemed miraculous, and if testified by travelers only as existing in China or Japan, would certainly have been disbelieved. The power of dipping the hand into melted metals unhurt, is a remarkable case of an effect of natural laws appearing to contravene another natural law; and it is one which certainly might have been, and probably has been regarded as a miracle and the fact believed or disbelieved, not according to the amount or quality of the testimony to it, but according to the credulity or supposed superior knowledge of the recipient. About twenty years ago, the fact that surgical operations could be performed on patients in the mesmeric trance without their being conscious of pain, was strenuously denied by most scientific and medical men in the country, and the patients, and sometimes the operators, denounced as impostors; the asserted phenomenon was believed to be contrary to the laws of nature ...

"We know so little of what nerve or life-force really is, how it acts or can act, and in what degree it is capable of transmission from one human being to another, that it would be indeed

rash to affirm that under no exceptional conditions could phenomena, such as the apparently miraculous cure of many diseases, or perceptions through other channels than the ordinary
senses, ever take place ... It is possible that intelligent beings
may exist, capable of acting on matter, though they themselves
are uncognisable directly by our senses."

Sitting in my aluminum boat, I wondered what made this
most rational of nineteenth-century minds so willing to concede the existence of the supernatural. Perhaps there was something about the age – something in the air, maybe – that lent
itself to such paradox.

Similarly, while Alfred Russel Wallace wrestled with the scientific versus the supernatural, Mary Baker Eddy was coming
to terms with the same conundrum. After a serious fall in
Lynn, Massachusetts, in February of 1866, Eddy claimed she
found in Matthew 9:2 of the Bible the key to spiritual healing. "It is plain to me," she would later write of "discovering" Christian Science, "that God does not employ drugs or
hygiene, nor provide them for human use; else Jesus would
have recommended and employed them in his healing.... The
tender word and Christian encouragement of an invalid, pitiful
patience with his fears and the removal of them, are better than
hecatombs of gushing theories, stereotyped borrowed speeches,
and the doling of arguments, which are but so many parodies
on legitimate Christian Science, aflame with divine love."

It was clear to me, sitting in the aluminum boat, that a
deeply rooted disposition toward irrational thinking strangely
cohabitated with the scientific theories of Darwin and Pasteur.
As Captain Red Beard revved the engine, I looked at the north
end of McNab's Island and scanned the shoreline. As I did, it
occurred to me that the local fears of Fenians, Confederation,
and cholera were much like the fear of Glaisher's blue mist.
Each seemed more a symptom or symbol of a deeper fear – a
fear of fate.

Perhaps not by coincidence, in 1860, just a few years before the outbreak of the fourth cholera epidemic, American philosopher Ralph Waldo Emerson pondered the outer limits of the human spirit and its creative genius. In his essay "Fate," he argued that our human character is best defined in that moment when the freedom of our spirit met the finality of our fate. "The secret of the world," he wrote, "is the tie between person and event. Person makes event, and event person."

The more I thought about this the more I wondered if our present age was any different than the mid-nineteenth century. Given our own obsessions with blue mists – with Islamic terrorists and superbugs, rogue states and nuclear annihilation – might not these emigrants from Germany and Ireland, and the common citizens of Halifax, all occupying a unique time and space in the spring of 1866, and all facing their own miasmic blue mists, have some useful wisdom to offer us in the present – a present equally enshrouded in its own blue mist? And I wondered, too: what might this story – this tale of a death ship in Halifax Harbour – have to say to us about the limits of human agency in the face of fate?

As the boat pulled away from the wharf, and the push of the engine lifted the bow off the water, I thought one final time about Emerson and about his long meditation on fate. "Nature is no sentimentalist," he wrote. "The world is rough and surly, and will not mind drowning a man or woman; but will swallow your ship like a grain of dust. The diseased, the elements, fortune, gravity, lightning, respect no persons." Pondering this, I considered the possible answers to my questions.

And in doing so, my thoughts turned to two young men – one, an Iranian bricklayer who walked lazily through the streets of Tehran; and the other, a German immigrant who sat pensively on a steamship in New York Harbor – and to the tangential connection, a whole world apart, that bound together their individual fates.

2

Causes of Attack

"CAUSES OF ATTACK – I have personally investigated at least a hundred cases, and not less than three-fourths could be traced directly to improper diet, or to intoxicating drinks, or to both united. Of the remainder, suppressed perspiration would comprise a large number. A strong, healthy, temperate labouring man had a severe attack of cholera, and after the danger had passed I was curious to ascertain the cause. He had been cautious and prudent in his diet. He used nothing intoxicating. His residence was in a good locality. But after some hours of hard labour and very profuse perspiration, he had lain down to take his customary nap right against an open window through which a very refreshing wind was blowing. Another cause is drinking largely of cold water when hot and thirsty. Great fatigue, great anxiety, fright, fear, all figure among inciting causes. If one can avoid all these he is as safe from the cholera as from being swept away by a comet."

– Dr. Cyrus Hamlin, Constantinople, 1865

Captain Red Beard's boat cut deftly from Fisherman's Cove and darted out across the channel, turning left in a broad, sweeping arc that brought us around the north end of Lawlor's Island. It then turned full toward the west, where the eastern breadth of McNab's Island greeted us with its broad swath of green and gentle hints of early autumn yellow, red, and brown. From the Eastern Passage side, the island – almost five kilometres long and as much as a kilometre and a half wide – presented itself as a series of low, rolling hills, geographic formations called drumlins, half-egg shaped hills of red clay. Here, on the Dartmouth side of the harbour, that clay is called the Lawrencetown Till, and was carved and shaped by a vast retreating ice sheet, known as the Wisconsin Glacier, over thousands of years, sometime between 20,000 and 10,000 B.C.E. – more or less.

Naturally, the shape of McNab's Island by the time the Wisconsin Glacier disappeared was much different than it is today. In fact, it wasn't an island at all, as sea levels were roughly sixty-five metres lower, leaving the mainland shoreline about a dozen kilometres southeast of the present-day island. At the same time, as the glacial ice retreated, portions of the Earth's mantle were released from the great weight of the ice and the earth lifted. This meant that, over the course of the last 10,000 years, the land that became McNab's Island both rose in places and settled in others.

Concurrent with this rising and falling was the reasonably fast – in geological terms, anyway – rising of the ocean. Vast stretches of melting ice, as one would expect, raised water levels considerably, creating both the Halifax Harbour and, ultimately, McNab's Island, a process that continues to this day. Rising sea levels due to climate change continue to alter the island's shape, as do regular North Atlantic storms that buffet its shoreline. In fact, the shoreline at McNab's southern end is said to be eroding at the astonishing rate of two and a half metres a year.

With Lawlor's Island behind us, Captain Red Beard's boat made its way toward a narrow beach, to a place called Back Cove by some and Wreck Cove by others. There, in the sandy shallows, the aluminum boat slowed and then came to an abrupt stop. Moving from his seat in the boat, Captain Red Beard jumped confidently into the water and hauled the nose of the boat up onto the beach, where, following the captain's invitation, I demonstrated my own skillful seamanship by lurching awkwardly toward the bow and then nearly falling off the boat's edge onto the sand. Even when I managed to get onto the beach, I artfully stumbled again and nearly tossed my blue nylon backpack and black fleece jacket into the water.

When I finally recovered my balance – and something of my dignity – Captain Red Beard and I stood on the sun-bleached sand and casually talked. After a time, the captain offered me something of a set speech on the island's sites and rules. He pointed out – on a small, pale-blue map that he produced for the island day tripper – the three remaining private residences (which were, apparently, to be assiduously avoided), and then he moved onto an odd, though thoroughly amusing, discussion about the inherent unfairness of the modern tax system. When he finished, I seized the initiative and suggested that we meet here again at the day's end.

The captain agreed.

So, with nothing more to say, I slid my pack over my shoulder, pulled my Red Sox hat onto my head, and offered a hearty thanks. Then I set off, outwardly intrepid, on a path that snaked through a sand dune covered in beach grass and then turned sharply right and upward onto a narrow stone and mud trail that disappeared into the woods. At the point where the trail made its dash from the dune to the trees, I stopped and watched over my shoulder as Captain Red Beard climbed back into his boat, fired up his engine, and turned the bow back toward Fisherman's Cove.

At once, I felt unnervingly alone with more than just a tinge of anxiety creeping up my spine. Yet, with my muse still calling – and frankly, since I had little choice but to spend the whole day – I feigned fearlessness, adjusted my shoulder straps, and plunged headlong into the forest. After all, I had the past to find.

The forest trail quickly widened to a four-foot lane of dirt and rock with a narrow, grassy strip running down the centre. For a time, I ambled along this path in a slow serpentine manner, stepping with care around misshapen black-brown mud puddles that pockmarked the way. As I moved, I tried to enter into the spirit of my quest by imagining something of Halifax's long past and specifically by imagining the tone and flavour of late March, 1866, just a few days before the arrival, on the other side of this island, of a cholera ship. But puddle-jumping wasn't conducive to such efforts, so I stopped on a mostly dry spot and removed my shoulder bag. Unzipping the main pouch, I rummaged about and removed a few sheets of paper from a red file folder: photocopies of *The Halifax Citizen* newspaper for Saturday, March 24, 1866.

I turned the sheets upright and read with some amuse-ment of Thomas Flinn, who was "charged with having broken a pane of glass in the store of M.H. Wetherby," and of Dennis Dolliver who was "charged with fighting and creating a distur-bance on the street." So, too, I noted an intriguing tale from Lunenburg, where "some persons were engaged in card-playing in a house at Conquerall Bank. Intoxicating liquor, the usual accompaniment of card-playing, was freely used. A school-teacher and a lad had some words in reference to their game, when the teacher jumped up, clinched the lad by the throat, who in return threatened to stab his opponent unless he relin-quished his hold. This request not being complied with, the boy stuck his knife into the man in several places – one stab between the ribs nearly proved fatal. His life is despaired of."

In yet another section of the paper, I followed the ongoing story of the Fenian scare. "A considerable number of citizens of the United States now resident in this city," the *Citizen* reported, "the large majority of them Southerners, last week tendered their services to the Governor for defense of the City and Province against Fenians or other filibusters having designs upon us. The Governor replied in handsome terms, stating that their services were accepted and would be employed if occasion required. Colonel Jones' Brigade of Militia Artillery, numbering eight hundred and forty-seven men, have been drilling daily through the week. The men are all in uniform, and are pronounced to be in a high state of efficiency. One man was dismissed for refusing to take the oath of allegiance; he was stripped of his uniform by Captain Kenny, and drummed out of the ranks. He will likely be looked after sharply. Col. Duvar's Brigade, the Third, is also in a high state of efficiency. The various detachments at Fort Clarence and York Redoubt passed a creditable inspection yesterday and to-day.

"It seems," continued the report, "the rumour about the [Fenian] bombardment of Yarmouth current here four days ago, has been quite excelled by the stories circulating elsewhere. In one rural locality it was asserted and generally believed that there was a fleet of sixty vessels loaded with Fenians off Halifax Harbour. In some places families are afraid to retire at night, without a sentry to give the alarm in case of a night attack; and we have heard of one prudent defender of the country who refuses to go to sleep at night without an axe beside his pillow, that being the nearest approach to an offensive or defensive weapon that he has at command."

As I finished reading the section, I pulled my rucksack back over my shoulder and, still holding the papers in my hand, ambled off again, dodging puddles with the grace of a gazelle – blind and wounded. As I walked, I mused about the tangible nervousness that must have existed among the citizens of Halifax in March of 1866 and about the perceived Fenian threat that added to the deep well of ethnic suspicion, already strong and sometimes dangerous, between the city's English and the Irish.

Halifax had a long history of Irish antipathy. At the city's inception in 1749, nearly two hundred Irish settlers – mostly labourers and servants – came ashore with English settlers. By 1760, nearly one-third of the city's 3,000 people were Irish. Most of those were Catholic. As the years passed, Irish immigration to the city continued to grow, with a second great wave of Irish immigrants coming in the mid 1830s. As was the case in so many North American cities, these Irish immigrants were hardly made to feel welcome, with many English Protestants regarding them with barely contained disdain and distrust.

Mind, this situation was the product of a long, difficult relationship between the English and the Irish stretching back for centuries, with the Irish suffering terribly under the oppressive, exploitive hand of the English. Certainly, the Fenian scare of early 1866 – encouraged and amplified by newspapers across North America – only reinforced such divisions and suspicions. "There are rumors circulating [in Baltimore]," reported *The New York Times* on March 11, 1866, "that a body of 800 fenians will leave here tomorrow evening by the Northern Central Railroad for Canada, or somewhere else."

I imagined the suspicious looks that passed between the city's English and Irish residents as I folded the photocopied newspapers in my hands into quarters, then tucked the sheets neatly into my jacket pocket. With my mind still pondering the city's Irish, I continued to wander down the rock and dirt path, which Captain Red Beard's map identified as the island's main route, called Garrison Road – a comically grandiose title for what was little more than a rutted, muddy trail.

And so I plodded on, passing to my right a thick patch of green ferns, which showed hints of yellow and brown. Behind these lay a thicket of stunted spruce, with narrow branches, twisted and mossy. Farther on, at my left, ran a dense coppice of elm trees and more stunted pines, interrupted now and again by brief clearings of high, yellow grass. Another fifty yards on, I encountered a wide swath of fallen, fast-rotting trees, ghostly reminders of Hurricane Juan that blew through Halifax in late 2003. And finally, after ambling along another few dozen yards, I caught my first sight of McNab's Pond.

Wide and shallow, McNab's Pond seemed notably devoid of life. Along its edges, the dark water gave way to thick stretches of churned-up, soupy marsh where leafless grey branches reached out of misshapen puddles into faintly miasmic air that smelled richly of rotted leaves and water too long still. Surveying this scene under the darkened grey skies, I was struck by the dank, netherworldly feel. As I looked toward the pond's edge and examined the fetid puddles, I found myself thinking again about the unseen central character of my tale: cholera.

I stopped and removed my shoulder bag again, placing it at my feet, and rummaged through the centre pocket. From inside the red folder, I removed two sheets, both copies of old photographs, and looked at them. The first, taken in the mid-1860s, was a picture of an Iranian bricklayer with a broad, flat nose and a thick, unkempt beard. In front of a grey backdrop of cloth, resting on a dirt floor or city street, he stood unnaturally erect. In his hands, he held the tools of his trade: a rounded, wooden mold or sieve; a long-handled, wooden shovel; and a four-legged wooden stool. On his head, he wore a simple, rimless woolen hat, while over his shoulders he had rested a grey woolen coat, covered in dust, torn and tattered at the ends. Notably, the bricklayer was barefoot.

Though I had no evidence of his life beyond the moment of this picture, I imagined him, in the stultifying heat of a summer's day, walking among the working poor of Tehran. So, too, I imagined him stepping through the narrow alleys and around the puddles that pockmarked the lanes, his movements upsetting the myriad flies that swarmed about his legs and head. I watched him wave them off and continue on, brushing and bumping against dozens of pilgrims who had come to Tehran on the hajj, the ritual trip to Mecca that Muslims committed themselves to at least once in their lifetimes. Tehran was a major intersection on the hajj route, from Europe to Mecca, and its markets and businesses thrived in the constant bustle of incoming and outgoing pilgrims. I let my imagination play further and watched the bricklayer step across an open water channel that snaked its way through the city streets like veins in a body.

These channels were called quantas, a form of aqueduct, which brought water to Tehran from great distances along streams and underground springs from the Elburz Mountains in the north. Mostly, the quantas were buried below the earth's surface, the water travelling beneath stone covers designed to reduce evaporation. Yet once the quantas entered the city limits – in cities like Bouroudijid, Muhanmmareh, Shushtar, and Tehran – the stone slabs were removed, offering a steady supply of water to all neighbourhoods, rich and poor.

Thinking about these water channels, I imagined a group of children cooling themselves by the quantas, splashing about in the rushing water. And I imagined a small gathering of women, situated just upstream from the playing children, as they knelt to wash clothing and bedding. I pictured one woman in particular as she scrubbed the shirt of a family member – a husband perhaps, or a brother-in-law, sick with cholera. Unseen by her as she washed the shirt, the cholera bacteria seeped into the quantas, and within moments, the microscopic creatures had washed over the children, who thought nothing of drinking the water as thirst came over them.

Still standing in sight of McNab's Pond, I looked for a time at the face of the Iranian bricklayer and wondered if perhaps his children were among those playing in the quantas, among those who consumed the cholera-contaminated water. Or perhaps it was his wife who had washed the clothes of his sick brother or uncle or father. I had no way of knowing, of course.

And yet, given the extent of the cholera epidemic in Iran in 1865, this bricklayer would have been touched in some way by the epidemic. He would have known someone who had become ill and died. I looked over the photograph in my hand and considered the travels of cholera in late 1865 through early 1866, from the alleyways of Tehran to the shores of McNab's Island. And then I considered the origins of cholera itself.

The cholera bacteria had existed for centuries before the nineteenth-century epidemics, first emerging in India along the well-used and well-populated banks of the Ganges River. Year after year, with each rainy season – and given the poor sanitary conditions of the time – the cholera bacteria would wax and wane. Yet, in 1817, the cholera took advantage of the expanding trade and military excursions of the British, travelling with sailors and soldiers on ships and caravans that pushed into territories where the disease had previously been without a foothold, such as Nepal and Afghanistan. By the 1820s, British ships had brought cholera to East Africa, China, and beyond. The results were catastrophic.

"How strange it is," wrote historian Dadabha Naoroji in 1901 in reference to the cholera epidemics, "that the British rulers do not see that, after all, they themselves are the main cause of the destruction that ensues from droughts; that it is the drain of India's wealth by them that lays at their own door the dreadful result of misery, starvation, and deaths of millions … Why blame poor Nature when the fault lies at your own door?"

The first cholera pandemic from 1816-1826 followed the British from India to China and to the edge of the Caspian Sea before finally exhausting itself. The second pandemic, from 1829 to 1851, travelled along a similar route but pushed much farther, finding fertile ground in Europe and North America where even Halifax experienced the epidemic in 1832, suffering the deaths of 600 citizens. The third cholera pandemic, from 1852 through 1862, focused itself largely in Russia, though outbreaks occurred elsewhere as far away as London and Chicago. And the fourth pandemic, beginning in 1863, emerged along the edges of Africa and the Middle East. For two years, the fourth cholera epidemic remained largely contained until it found a new means of mass mobility in the spring and summer of 1865: the annual Muslim pilgrimage to Mecca called the hajj.

By 1865 the once prohibitive costs and dangers of the trip to Mecca had abated with better travel conditions and the advent of more efficient trains and boats. For the first time in history, Muslim pilgrims of modest means could make the traditional trek. Of course, with the greater number of travellers came the unintended confluence and dispersion of cholera. The cholera bacteria that ultimately reached the shores of McNab's Island began its long journey in the sands of Persia, travelling to Mecca and returning with pilgrims to Europe and beyond.

The hajj pilgrims often began their journey to Mecca through Constantinople, where they travelled by boat across the Black Sea to the ports of Trabzon and Batum. From there they rode trains along the edge of the Caspian Sea, through Tiflis to Baku. After resting for a time in Baku, the pilgrims continued by ship to the port of Enzeli, where they trekked overland, under the heat of a Persian sun, to Qazvin and then to Tehran. Here, again, many pilgrims rested. When ready, they continued overland by long caravans to Baghdad and Karbala and Najaf. From Najaf, the pilgrims undertook a perilous trip across the Arabian Desert on what was called the "mountain caravan" to Ha'el. Then, when they had recovered from that arduous journey, the pilgrims began another long, dangerous caravan through the Arabian Desert to Mecca.

When cholera first emerged in the region, in the intensely hot spring and summer of 1865, 15,000 pilgrims died in Mecca. In Egypt, another 60,000 perished. And before the epidemic ran its course, from Turkey into central Europe, and from central Europe to England and then North America in 1866, more than 200,000 people had succumbed to the disease. "Europe realized," wrote Dr. Achille Proust, a professor of Hygiene at the University of Paris, in 1873, "that it could not remain like this, every year, at the mercy of the pilgrimage to Mecca."

Still holding the two photographs, I walked along Garrison Road, thinking about the Iranian bricklayer and the hajj pilgrims, until I reached the north end of McNab's Pond. There I turned left and strolled out along another narrow mud and rock lane called Lighthouse Road.

For many years, this narrow path arched its way gently westward from the body of the island to a rocky promontory on which sat a stout, circular stone building, called a Martello tower. Originally built in 1814, this Martello tower was outfitted with cannons positioned to defend the harbour. In 1826, practical minds recognized that the tower was well-suited for use as a lighthouse – though it was never fully abandoned as a military outpost – and a copula was built on top to accommodate a nightly flame. The tower may well have offered nothing more to local history had it not also been used in 1851 by Dr. Abraham Gesner for experiments that led to the discovery of kerosene, one of the life's blood – along with oil – of modern society.

In any event, despite its tough stone exterior, the Martello tower's exposed face was regularly subjected to rough Atlantic storms. And in 1931 a particularly fearsome storm did significant damage to the tower, leaving many to worry about its sturdiness. Rather than being repaired, the tower was simply left to deteriorate, until it was unceremoniously dismantled at the end of World War Two to make way for an unimaginative, modern cement lighthouse, which remains standing today, automated and lonely.

With the hope of standing at the lighthouse's base, I walked along the path, travelling about a third of the way along, until the road abruptly ended, roughly washed away by fierce waves churned up from Hurricane Juan. These same hurricane waves had also tossed large boulders willy-nilly about the cove, tearing another enormous hole farther up the road. So, unable to walk on, I looked to my left, over a brackish swamp called Hangman's Marsh, which was just an extension of McNab's Pond, to the land that runs along the opposite side, a stretch of small stones and sand called Hangman's Beach. There, many years in the past, pirates and criminals were hanged from a gibbet for their crimes. Often as not, the poor souls were left hanging, twisting slowly in the wind at the business end of the hangman's rope as a gruesome, medieval-style reminder of what befell criminals in that age of rough royal justice.

After pondering the gloominess of Hangman's Beach and Hangman's Marsh, I wandered back along Lighthouse Road, until I reached the junction with Garrison Road. There I turned left and meandered past another long stretch of green and yellow ferns, followed by another grove of elm and spruce trees. Farther on, the groves gave way to another low grass dune that rolled down to a sandy beach rimming McNab's Cove.

I ambled still farther until I reached the midway point of the cove where, jutting out into the calm water, there sat the weathered Government Wharf. On impulse, I turned from the road and strolled out to its end, where I took the bag from my shoulder and placed it by my side. With the sheets of paper still in my hand, I sat cross-legged on the wooden planks. Then, I tucked the image of the Iranian bricklayer behind the next.

The second sheet was a faded photograph of three people, taken sometime in the last decade of the nineteenth century. It captured a moment in the life of three German emigrants: Henry Wenner and his two sisters, Mary and Margaret. In the picture, the two sisters sat upright in the foreground, shoulder-to-shoulder. Mary was younger than Henry by two years, while Margaret was five years older. Despite the age difference, the sisters looked similar, both wearing stern, unsmiling faces with dark hair pulled back into tight, unseen buns. For this formal photograph, they wore dour black dresses with high collars buttoned to the throat. Around their necks, they hung thick crucifixes.

Behind the sisters stood Henry, erect with shoulders back, wearing a white shirt, grey tie, and black vest and coat. His hair was medium-short and brushed back, revealing a strong, broad forehead. A long, full beard obscured much of his face, yet his eyes were piercing and fierce, suggesting intense determination. Looking at those eyes, I imagined Henry as a young man on May 7, 1866. In the afternoon of that day, Henry was aboard the Steamship *Louisa May*, which was anchored in the narrows between Fort Hamilton and Staten Island at the mouth of New York Harbor. Its crew and passengers were waiting patiently, though nervously, for the local health officer to lift the quarantine that would allow the ship to enter the harbour.

Walking about the *Louisa May*'s deck were the survivors of a horrific cholera outbreak that occurred aboard a ship that was anchored off McNab's Island in Halifax Harbour. Below deck on the *Louisa May* sat Henry, holding a pen firmly in his hand just above a flat piece of light-yellow paper. For some time he hesitated, considering the words he would use in this letter to his parents, long anxious for some word. Then finally, with a deep breath and a determined air, he put pen to paper and began. "My dearly beloved parents," he wrote, "it is with joy that I take my pen to write you these lines. I had feared I might never be able to do so." Henry then thought back, some three weeks before the horror, to the moment of anticipation when his impending trip to New York meant the start of a new life.

Henry, nineteen, and his sisters, seventeen and twenty-four, had just left their home in Luxembourg along with three others from their village. As with so many, they had decided that the Old World no longer held the future they sought. So they agreed to emigrate to America. Being from a family of some means, Henry and his sisters engaged an agent, who had arranged passage from Luxembourg to America. "At six o'clock on the evening of the 24th of March," Henry recalled, "we arrived at Antwerp [Belgium], where the agent took us to a hotel. There we partook of our evening meal and remained until two o'clock the next morning, when we went about the ship."

Sitting on Government Wharf overlooking McNab's Cove, I imagined the conversations that Henry and his sisters had on that Saturday night. I heard them speak of Antwerp and of the journey ahead. If they slept that night, it was only for a few hours. "At five o'clock we embarked," Henry said. Though with some dark foreshadowing he also recalled, "All was fine until noon, when we fell victims to sea sickness, which lasted until we reached Hartlepool, England. This lasted from the 25th to the 27th of March, and was so bad that we couldn't eat. My sister Margaret was much more sick than I was." In Liverpool, Henry rented rooms for himself and his sisters.

While Henry and his sisters slept in their rooms, Patrick and Mary Healy had also left their home in Castlebar, County Mayo, Ireland, with Patrick's father and their four children – Patrick, Thomas, Bridget, and Mary. Together they travelled by train in crowded passenger cars to the port of Queenstown, some fifteen miles south and east of Cork. As with Henry Wenner and his sisters, they too followed the path of many millions before them who turned their backs on the difficult past and challenging future of their home country to immigrate to America and a new life.

Travelling, too, was a young Dutchman named Pieter De Jong, Jr. who made his way by ship from Liverpool to Queenstown, Ireland, with his brothers Elbert, Dirk, and Neldus, Dirk's wife Martinus and their youngest child, Arie. And there was Reverend Ambrose Martin, who planned to travel to America in comfort, as a saloon passenger in first class; and John

Thomas Griffith, his pregnant sister Catherine, her husband Evan Jones, and their niece; and Aris Eelman and his cousin Klaas Vlaming, who came from the Dutch island of Texel and had travelled to Rotterdam and then to Hull, England, where they boarded a train for Liverpool. And there was Oliver Bacon Harden, who travelled with his brothers Harry and Ed, all sons of John Walter Harden, who had sent for his family after he had immigrated to America a few years before. No doubt all of these emigrants, and the many hundreds of others who were making their way to the fated ship, were filled with the great promise of a future in America.

From my bag on the wharf, I removed a few more papers from the red folder, including two drawings of a mid-nineteenth-century steamship. For a time, I imagined Henry and his sisters, the Healy family, the De Jong family, Aris Eelman and Klaas Vlaming, the Harden brothers, and Reverend Martin as they arrived in Queenstown, Ireland, with more than a thousand other emigrants. And I imagined their impressions when, for the first time, they saw the ship that would take them all to America.

She was called the S.S. *England*.

3

Symptoms of an Attack

"SYMPTOMS OF AN ATTACK – While cholera is prevalent in a place, almost everyone experiences more or less disturbance of digestion. It is doubtless in part imaginary. Everyone notices the slightest variation of feeling, and this gives an importance to mere trifles. There is often a slight nausea, or transient pains, or rumbling sounds when no attack follows. No one is entirely free from these. But when diarrhea commences, though painless and slight, it is in reality the skirmishing party of the advancing column. It will have at first no single characteristic of Asiatic cholera. But do not be deceived. It is the cholera nevertheless. Wait a little, give it time to get hold, say to yourself, 'I feel perfectly well, it will soon pass off,' and in a short time you will repent of your folly in vain. I have seen many a one commit suicide in this way. Sometimes, though rarely, the attack commences with vomiting.

"But in whatever way it commences, it is sure to hold on. In a very few hours the patient may sink into the collapse. The hands and feet become cold and purplish, the countenance,

at first nervous and anxious, becomes gloomy and apathetic, although a mental restlessness and raging thirst torment the sufferer while the powers of life are ebbing. The intellect remains clear, but all the social and moral feelings seem wonderfully to collapse with the physical powers. The patient knows he is to die, but cares not a snap about it. In some cases, though rarely, the diarrhea continues for a day or two, and the foolish person keeps about, then suddenly sinks, sends for a physician, and before he arrives, 'dies as the fool dieth.'"
– Dr. Cyrus Hamlin, Constantinople, 1865

Still sitting cross-legged at the end of Government Wharf, I looked up and sighed. In the distance, I could see Mauger's Beach lighthouse and, swimming low in the calm water of the cove, a loon, heading west toward the harbour's mouth.

I returned my attention to the papers in my hand and reviewed the news of Wednesday, March 28, 1866. *The Halifax Citizen* reported that fifteen-month-old Ida McKie and two-year-old Margaret Cecilia, "the youngest daughter of Capt. James and Ellen O'Brien," had died of whooping cough. Two-month-old Abbie J. Hector had also died, of causes unknown. Elsewhere, thirty-four-year-old George Brehan succumbed to an illness after a ten-day fight, "which he bore with Christian fortitude, in the firm hope of a glorious immortality." And Margaret Ann Burnham had passed away in her forty-third year, "leaving a husband and six children to mourn her loss." At Ryerson's wharf, "a man named John Hubbard fell from the main boom of [the] Schooner, *Dispatch*, and perished. His body was recovered. He was about twenty-four years of age, and belonged to Wood's Harbour." Still, not all was fear and gloom in the city. The newspaper noted that "the show of beef cattle for Easter in the street to-day has been nearly as fine as in any previous year. Two or three of the oxen are marvels of size, symmetry, and fatness."

On the same day, in Liverpool, England, at "about noon [on Wednesday] of the 28th of March," Henry, Mary, and Margaret Wenner "boarded the large, ocean going steamer." Though Henry did not indicate whether his party was travelling first class or third class, he was clearly impressed by the size of the S.S. *England*. "This vessel was 370 feet long and fifty feet wide," he noted. I imagined the Wenners milling among the crowds gathered at the Liverpool dock that day, the German and Dutch emigrants – parents, grandparents, children, brothers, cousins, uncles and aunts – carrying bags and conversing loudly, their bodies funnelling together as they moved slowly toward the wooden gangplanks. For nearly six hours that day, this chaotic scene played itself out as the passengers, crew, and cargo filled the ship. Then, when the cargo was stored and passengers had boarded and were settled, Captain Grace ordered the steamship *England* to sea. According to *The Times* of London, the S.S. *England* "left the Mersey on the 28th of March at six o'clock in the evening."

I glanced up from my papers and could still see the loon, receding slowly into the distance. I turned to my right and looked across the cove to the bluff called Hugonin Point, which rose sharply from the water, its grass and brush turning an autumnal yellow. To the right of Hugonin Point lay Findlay's Cove, whose shoreline recessed for a few dozen yards before curving back and rejoining McNab's Cove. From there, my eyes followed the sand and rock beach south to a spot about twenty yards to my right, where in my mind's eye I saw, jutting out over the mostly placid water, another wharf called Findlay's Wharf. Though nothing remains of Findlay's Wharf today, save perhaps the rotted stumps of wooden pylons embedded in the sand below the surface, I tried to imagine the ship anchored there in early April of 1866 – the S.S. *England*.

To create an accurate image, I looked down again and reshuffled my papers until I came across two pictures of the steamship. Both were drawings – dramatic renderings, in fact – of the vessel at sea. The first was a black and white likeness: the *England* gliding smoothly on rough waters with the sails of three masts billowing, its single centre funnel spewing thick smoke. Tied high atop the main mast was the Union Jack, snapping sharply in the wind. The second picture was similar in presentation, though more dramatic rendered in colour. It, too, showed the S.S. *England* gliding smoothly across rough seas with billowing sails, a smoking funnel, and a snapping flag. This picture, however, was clearly designed for advertising. As such, it was framed with broad, curling designs and flanked by waving flags of Great Britain and the United States. On its top, the poster announced the "S.S. *England*" a proud part of the "National Line Steamships."

The S.S. *England* was, as another advertisement noted, "a well appointed ship" built in 1865 by Palmer Bros. & Co. at Jarrow-on-Tyne. Enormous for the age, she weighed 3,308 gross tons and stretched to 375.5 feet long, "with a clipper stem, a funnel, three masts, and a single screw." Her movement was impressive, travelling "at a speed of ten knots." Officially, she accommodated eighty first-class passengers and 800 third-class passengers. "These passenger Steamers," said a contemporary advertisement, "have been constructed in the best manner, at the most celebrated ship yards in Great Britain. They are built of iron and steel, in watertight and fireproof compart-ments, are of unusual strength and power, and [are] magnifi-cently equipped. They are rated among the finest in the World. As these Steamers are of the largest class, and of remarkable steadiness at Sea, Passengers are not so liable to sickness or discomforts."

The National Steam Navigation Company, the builders of the S.S. *England*, was based in Liverpool, England. Founded in 1863, it was established with the expressed intention of transporting cargo to the southern United States. But the advent of the American Civil War forced the company to alter its U.S. destination to New York City.

In truth, these new iron screw steamers were designed to capitalize on Europe's fastest growing export of the mid-nineteenth century – its emigrants. And a lucrative business it was. Between 1870 and 1900, more than twelve million immigrants travelled to the United States. And between 1860 and 1880, the vast majority of these emigrants came from England, Germany, and Ireland. The demand for ships travelling to the United States was such that, despite the rapid building of such human cargo vessels, most ships at the time were regularly filled beyond capacity.

Certainly, this was true for the *England*. On March 28, 1866, the three Wenners ascended the gangplank in Liverpool with 500 or 600 others, after which the ship sailed for Queenstown, Ireland, where she took on an additional 700 passengers, far more than was allowed by the design of the ship or the regulations of the time.

I looked up again from the drawings and focused intently on my imagined ship in the cove. In my mind's eye, I carefully measured out her length, acquiring a vague sense of the great size. I imagined her tall masts, her large funnel, and her broad wooden deck. On this deck, I imagined the entrance to steep stairs that descended below to the first-class accommodations for saloon passengers. By careful design, these passengers were lavished with modern comforts.

"The saloons and staterooms are very spacious and cheerful," announced one shipbuilder's description, "finely lighted and ventilated, and elegantly furnished. The [dining] table will compare favorably with that of the best hotels in England. [Also provided are] Ladies Boudoir, Piano, Smoking, and Bath Rooms, etc. A Surgeon, Stewards, and Stewardesses on every

Steamer. Medicine and attendance free." Contemporary newspaper accounts similarly described the saloons: "The between deck has a height of eight feet. The ventilation is extremely good, and it is equipped in an excellent way in all matters. It can be safely recommended as a … good passenger ship."

I pictured a sleek, narrow room, with wide, comfortable berths on either side of a porcelain washbasin topped by a wood-framed mirror. Then, again in my mind's eye, I left the room and walked along the saloon deck until I came across another staircase entrance and descended. On this next deck, I found the hold of the third-class passengers.

Here passengers were provided more modest accommodations, though the ship's builders were careful to suggest otherwise. "The steerage is large, light and airy," promised one advertisement, "and warmed by steam in winter. Married couples and families are berthed together; single persons placed in separate rooms. Meals are served regularly three times a day by the Ship's Stewards, and consist of an unlimited quantity of good and wholesome provisions, put on board under the inspection of the Company's Purveyor. Plenty of fresh drinking water. The care of Surgeon and Stewards free." For propriety's sake, single women were located in bunks at the fore of the ship while single men were situated in the aft. Married couples and families occupied the centre.

Contemporary drawings of steerage quarters suggested something less than advertised. Situated above the storage deck, the third-class steerage deck had a ceiling height of just six feet. Along the walls were a series of rough, wooden bunks, each wide enough for three to six people. These bunks were designed for occupants to lie in the direction of the moving ship, though on some vessels the bunks cut across the deck, allowing for more passengers, but causing greater discomfort and sickness on rough voyages.

When not sleeping in their bunks, third-class passengers had little more to do than sit in the long narrow corridor or walk about the tight quarters. At the best of times, the accommodations were dark and crowded. The only source of light and air came from the hatches to the decks above, which were often covered by simple canvases. During rough seas or storms, these canvases would be replaced by sturdy wooden covers that would not allow for the free flow of air. As such, in long periods of inclement weather, the battened-down hatches created poor, even dangerous, conditions.

The facilities and food of third-class also left something to be desired. Third-class passengers in need of a bathroom found two rudimentary privies located on either side of the ship. Given the number of passengers on board, long lines often stretched from the privy, down the narrow corridors, and past the crowded bunks.

Another contemporary drawing showed that food was served from waist-high cauldrons located near the centre of the ship, in the same space as the bathrooms. At mealtimes, passengers would pour soup or gruel into cups or onto plates. The drawing suggested that, when the ship pitched roughly on the rolling waves, passengers would fall into one another, dropping food onto the deck and each other. Given the food, the bathrooms, and the passengers in tight quarters, the smells must have been overwhelming. Indeed, this pungency was remembered by many who also noted the absolute darkness at night and the endless sounds of heavy breathing, quiet conversation, and coughing. "When we had boarded the ship," said one passenger, "we were shown our berths, the only place where we could stay while we were between decks. There were two berths on top of each other, and in front of them we had a little space where we could eat our food."

Another passenger noted, "[O]ur place as emigrants was in the hold, on the between deck. Everyone had a chest of food, a keg of milk and one of beer, all of which was stored in the middle of the deck, held in place by ropes." No doubt the passengers did their best to stay cheerful. Those who were religious looked to prayer. And those with musical talents shared lively tunes played on fiddles and squeezeboxes, while other passengers danced and sang the time away.

Of course, such crossings were not without tragedies. On one ship, an emigrant remembered the death of a child. "A boy did die on the Atlantic. I will never forget the funeral," recalled the emigrant. "The ship's carpenter made a coffin of rough planks, and filled it with sand in the bottom. Then he bored holes in the side to make it sink faster. But it did not sink fast, and as the wood in the coffin had a pale colour we could watch for a long time as it was slowly sinking."

Shifting my position on the Government Wharf, I considered the conversations among the emigrants, as the ship moved through the night of Thursday, March 28, 1866, and then arrived the next morning at the port of Queenstown, Ireland. There, gathered on the waterfront, in full view of the long row of colourful three- and four-storey houses, stood nearly 800 Irish emigrants preparing to board. Henry Wenner and his sisters likely watched the proceedings from the top deck. Noted Henry, "Quite a few emigrants from Ireland were taken aboard." As he remembered it, "In all, there were 1,300 persons." The London *Times* reported that the S.S. *England* "had then over 1,000 passengers, of whom 400 were Germans, on board." Whichever number was correct, it was clear that the ship was overcrowded – except perhaps for those sailing first-class.

"I was a saloon passenger on board the unfortunate steamship *England*," later wrote Reverend Ambrose Martin, "which sailed from Liverpool on the 28th day of March." Amid the comfort of the first-class accommodations, Reverend Martin enjoyed himself as he watched the German and English passengers board in Liverpool. "We left full of health, joy and hope, and reached Queenstown on the following evening, the

29th, about 5 o'clock. We embarked our passengers, and waved a farewell to our friends left behind." However, such health, joy, and hope were not to last long.

Late on March 29, under a near cloudless sky and on gently rolling seas, the S.S. *England* set sail for New York. The mood by all accounts was festive, with more than a thousand emigrants filled with the promise of new lives in a new land. "We had a very stiff breeze during our stay and while leaving Queenstown," noted Reverend Martin. "That night all was hurry, but not confusion, in taking possession of our respective berths, and making our various domestic arrangements for the voyage. Next morning was fine and calm, and all arose full of health and strength."

Soon after the S.S. *England* left Queenstown, however, the weather changed. Over the next three days, on March 30, 31, and April 1, "on Good Friday, Saturday and Easter Sunday," remembered Henry Wenner, "we encountered a terrific storm." Remembered another of the conditions below deck, "[T]he poor people were closed down without a breath of air." Seasickness among the third-class passengers spread quickly and with it came much vomiting.

Thumbing through more papers on the wharf, I noted that back in Halifax, on Thursday, March 29, 1866, "James Ballantyne was fined $20 for stealing a sum of money from Thomas Loyd," while Mark Aylward and Hugh Miller were "found drunk" and sent to the city prison for a week. James Sutherland was "fined one dollar for violating the Hack Ordnance by leaving his cab on the public stand, without an attendant" and "William Johnston (coloured) was charged with using obscene language on the street, admonished and dismissed." So, too, George Cook, Samuel Cook, George Taylor, George Demons, John Taylor and George Tolliver were all "charged with creating a disturbance on the street" and "fined one dollar or one week each [in the] city prison." In Queens County, the paper reported, "eighteen persons have died of Diphtheria since autumn."

Keeping the Fenian fear alive, *The Halifax Citizen* reported, "Some days ago when the Fenian excitement was at its height a Company of Eighty Volunteers were formed in the Town of Windsor in four hours, and when Colonel Laurie came up to inspect, the Militia marched to the ground. We learn that they comprise a very fair body of men who are now engaged in perfecting themselves in Drill and taking the preliminary steps previous to applying to the government for Arms. Colonel Jenkins of the Militia is forwarding the Company's interests in every way – their uniform has been sent for and we hope to see this Company soon uniformed – drilled and equipped for the defence of our Common Country."

While the emigrants on board the S.S. *England* endured the fearsome squall through the third day, Halifax, too, was "visited … by a severe storm of wind and rain," the intense weather lasting for nearly two hours through that afternoon. The wind blew "with unusual violence from the South, raising a heavy sea in the harbour, and causing some damage to vessels at the wharves." With the storm fast approaching, those working on the busy waterfront rushed about, lashing down items that might blow over.

Atop one wharf, called Strachen's, William Kennedy, a young boy of nine, played in a small dinghy. The boat was a playful source of movement for the boy as it rocked across the wooden planks in the wind – until a strong gust caught the underside of the boat and flipped it off the wharf and into the water. "As it fell, it turned bottom up," noted the newspaper, and there it "floated thus with the boy inside for a considerable time." In the chaos of the storm, with people running to and fro on the waterfront, no one was aware of the boy. And so, reported the paper, "no effort was made to save him."

After a time, the boat drifted into the dock and, amid the rolling waves, finally lifted enough to release the boy, who floated "out from under [the boat] and was picked up." The ensuing scene on the dock was rife with fear and panic. "To all appearance," said the paper, the boy was "dead." But those in attendance would not give up. They used the "usual measures ... to resuscitate him" and, miraculously, the boy revived, coughing and cold, but alive. As the newspaper later noted, perhaps with a sigh of relief, "we are glad to learn he is now out of danger." No doubt the citizens of Halifax were pleased that tragedy had been averted.

Their relief, however, would prove temporary.

4

For Stopping the Incipient Diarrhea

"FOR STOPPING THE INCIPIENT DIARRHEA – The mixture which I used in 1848 with great success, and again in 1855, has during this epidemic been used by thousands, and, although the attacks have been more sudden and violent, it has fully established its reputation for efficiency and perfect safety. It consists of equal parts by measure of 1) Laudanum and spirits of camphor, 2) Tincture of Rhubarb. In an adult, 30 drops on a lump of sugar will often check the diarrhea. But to prevent its return, care should always be taken to continue the medicine every four hours in diminishing doses of 25, 20, 15, 10, 9, when careful diet is all that is needed. In case the first does not stay the diarrhea continue to give in increasing doses, 35, 40, 45, 60, at every movement of the bowels. Large doses will produce no injury while the diarrhea lasts. When that is checked then is the time for caution. I have never seen a case of diarrhea taken in season which was not thus controlled, but some cases of advanced diarrhea, and especially of relapse, paid no heed to it whatever.

"As soon as this becomes apparent, I have always resorted to this course: Procure a teacup of starch boiled as for use in starching linen, and stir into it a full teaspoon of laudanum for an injection. Give one-third at each movement of the bowels. In one desperate case, abandoned as hopeless by a physician, I could not stop the diarrhea until the seventh injection, which contained nearly a teaspoonful of laudanum. The patient recovered, and is in perfect health. At the same time, I use prepared chalk in 12-grain doses, with a few drops of laudanum and camphor to each. But whatever course is pursued it must be followed up, and the diarrhea controlled or the patient is lost."
– Dr. Cyrus Hamlin, Constantinople, 1865

As I continued to read, a gust of wind rustled the papers in my hands. I glanced up and looked out across the cove. The clouds in the distance had thickened and turned a darker grey, while beneath me, the water rippled and lapped against the dock. I returned my newspapers to my bag, stood, and then slung the bag over my shoulder. Adjusting my hat, I retreated along Government Wharf to Garrison Road, where I turned left and headed north.

Quickly enough, I left sight of the cove and entered a loose tunnel of elms and ferns. Farther along, I rounded a bend and came upon a fork where Garrison Road split into the Old Military Road to the right and Garrison Road to the left. For no particular reason, I meandered to the right, into a thicket of green trees and glades of high, yellow grass, and continued on.

On Tuesday, April 2, 1866, the *Citizen* reported that George A. McLoad, a native of Scotland, died in his fifty-fourth year after a severe illness, and that Donald McDonald, aged forty-seven, and Mary Taggert, aged forty-nine, had also both died of a "short severe illness." At the city's poor asylum, Margaret Skinner, aged thirty-six years and a native of Halifax, passed on, while John Romans, the only son of George and Bella Romans, passed away at the age of ten months and eight days for reasons unsaid. And Sarah Taylor, aged thirty-three, died of typhoid fever, "leaving a husband and two children to mourn their loss." So, too, reported the paper, "Mr. Abel Forbes was driving a load of hay down a steep hill, the oxen took fright, and whilst trying to stop them he fell and the cart passed over his body. He was carried home, and his injuries were so severe that he lived only a few days."

At sea, Captain Douglass, of the brig *Adelaide*, reported that his ship, laden with molasses, left Cienfuegos, Cuba, bound to St. John's, Newfoundland. Along the way, she "was struck by a heavy squall … doing considerable damage. While clearing wreck[age] from hull the mate was taken overboard." The man, "after being in the water a long time was got on board in an almost exhausted condition." The ship was adrift and in great danger when, that afternoon, they "saw a vessel coming toward us under small sail. She proved to be the ship *E.C. Scranton*, Capt. Williams, from Liverpool for New York." The captain of that ship "launched his life boat, and with great difficulty succeeded in rescuing us from the wreck, saving nothing but what we stood in."

In Halifax, Daniel O'Leary was remanded to prison for "committing an assault upon his wife," while Jason White and James O'Conner were "fined one dollar each for going into the Police Station whilst in a state of intoxication." Elsewhere, "a lad named Benjamin Cox, was arraigned for playing ball in the street," while "Mary Kiely was fined four dollars for committing an assault upon Sophia Wiseman." Excused from punishment were "William Rawley and James Watt, who were charged with having thrown snowballs at persons in the street." Robert Torsey was "charged with stealing a pair of socks, of the value of 1s.3d. [1 shilling 3 pence]." He was "convicted and sentenced to pay a fine of $2 or 20 days in city prison." So, too, Ann Pritchard was "charged with wandering on the streets at an unreasonable hour," but she was "discharged on condition of leaving the city."

As precaution against the Fenian threat, "Heavy guns were mounted in Sydney, Cape Breton," while in Digby, the military erected "earth-works in the rear of the town, on which a 32 pounder is mounted, and five other guns are to be mounted at the north end. The *Daring* arrived there last Thursday with arms and ammunition for the militia." And in Hants County, "several men watched three nights for a mutton-loving brute," a "wild cat" that had "killed eighteen sheep in the district of Upper Kennetcook." The men, reported the newspaper, "succeeded in shooting him on the third night."

As I ambled along the path, I again thought about the S.S. *England* at sea. On her fourth day out from Liverpool, she continued to weather the fearsome Atlantic tempest. Throughout the storm, the third-class passengers suffered terribly, with an ever-increasing number succumbing to seasickness. The sounds of illness – the coughing, the crying, the moaning, and the vomiting – filled the near darkness of the third-class deck. And as the rough seas continued into April 2, matters only worsened. "Four days after leaving Queenstown," recalled Henry Wenner, "a boy was found dead alongside his mother."

Reverend Ambrose Martin remembered the death as well. "On the morning of the fourth day," he would later say, "after our departure from Queenstown, a young German boy, aged eight years, was found dead in his berth by the side of his mother." The scene must have been heartbreaking. I imagined the mother by flickering candlelight, sitting in her bunk, weeping inconsolably. She held her son tightly to her breast. I looked at the faces in the shadows of the nearby passengers, weak from seasickness, staring at the mother and son with a mixture of pity and fear.

After consoling the mother for a time, Reverend Martin gently took the dead child from her arms. With the aid of another man, he brought the body topside, where, after brief preparations, he performed a solemn ceremony. Then the boy, weighted down with iron, was buried at sea. "That night the wind was very strong and the sea rough," recalled Reverend Martin, "and our vessel rolled heavily. I performed the burial service over the child, and we then consigned his remains to the deep." After the burial, all returned grimly below deck to wait out the storm – until a second death occurred.

"The evening of the same day," remembered Rev. Martin, "I was called to the bedside of a fine, stout Irishman – Thomas Walsh, thirty-five years old." When Martin arrived at the bunk, Thomas Walsh was shaking. He complained "of cold feet, and cramps in the legs and stomach." Three doctors were attending to him. "All human aid was brought to bear on the poor writhing victim," recalled Martin, "but in vain – he died the next morning about 2:30 o'clock."

Many on board believed these deaths were the result of a rough Atlantic crossing. "Sickness," recounted Martin, "now set in with fearful severity." Martin found himself moving constantly through the ship. "My calls were continuous," he would later say. "The well passengers were awed, and questioned each other, as to the cause of this calamity, this awful visitation. The doctors were unremitting in their attention. Nothing was spared whether in skill, soothing or nourishment."

Still, others suspected the worst. "It was an overcrowded boat," recalled Oliver Bacon Harden. "The funerals became very frequent, and it was then known that the Cholera was sailing with us."

As the hasty burials increased, a deep fear permeated the ship. "Perhaps the first buried at sea we saw was a gruesome sight, as the coffin caught on the side of the ship, and the lid came off exposing the corpse," Oliver Bacon Harding remembered. "So many deaths took place that they used up all the wood and then they sewed them up in sacks." Not long afterward, Oliver and his brother Ed found that they too were ill.

Recalled Henry Wenner, suggesting something of the fear growing among the passengers and their desire for divine assistance, "We were most fortunate to have a priest always with us, so that all could receive the sacrament of penance, and die fortified by the sacrament of Extreme Unction. The name of the priest was Karolous Baum ... he is a native of Luxembourg." As the priest worked, the deaths continued to come. "As many as fifteen emigrants died in one day," remembered Henry Wenner.

At the same time, Patrick Healy and his family – his brothers, sister, mother, and father – all below deck among the third-class passengers suffered a terrible loss. "Everyone," recalled Patrick of the initial mood on the ship, "was singing and dancing, and having a merry time until a man took sick and was in violent pain and died. Then, next day, ten died; the following, fifty." And then "little Mary," Patrick's sister, "who was two years old at the time" contracted the illness and died. A priest administered the last rites and then, as Patrick noted, it was his "father who was appointed by the doctors to help wrap the body in sheets and slide [little Mary] out of the manhole into the ocean." Patrick remembered bitterly, "She was thrown overboard."

So, too, Pieter De Jong, who had boarded the S.S. *England* with his brothers Elbert, Neldus, Dirk, and Dirk's wife Martinus and their youngest child, Arie, watched with growing dread and deepening grief as each of his family members, in turn, became ill, suffered, and then died. Elsewhere, the pregnant Catherine Jones, with her son at her side, also watched as her husband Evan and then her niece both contracted the illness and died.

Of the conditions on the ship, Reverend Ambrose Martin remembered, "The officers on board from the commandant, Captain Grace, to the lowest servant vied with each other in their attendance on the sick. The food of the passengers was good, wholesome and abundant. Many laboured under seasickness, and the food appeared to them unpalatable. But to the weak a more delicate and suitable food was given, according to the means we had on board."

But Henry Wenner had a more sober assessment. "The food," he remembered, "was very poor from Liverpool to Halifax. The meat was more than half raw most of the time, and the potatoes very often. Many believed the sickness was contracted on shipboard, for there had been a disease among the cattle a few years before in England. Others thought it was caused by the cold. Again, others thought it was carried by the Germans." Henry's own observations suggested that the spread of the sickness among the different ethnic groups on board was otherwise. "The largest number [of victims]," he recalled, "were the Irish and Hollanders. There were not so many Luxembourgers."

Despite the heroic efforts of the doctors, priests, passengers, and crew, the deaths only continued and the number of ill only increased. "My sick calls were more frequent," recalled Reverend Martin, "and the deaths increased daily – sometimes eight, ten, twelve, or even fifteen, died in one day. Oh! What a Sight!"

And still the deaths mounted. As Aris Eelman noted, "I was there when fifty people died in one day and were thrown overboard like a cat or a dog."

I imagined these horrors witnessed by Reverend Martin and Henry Wenner as I continued wandering along Old Military Road, until my thoughts were interrupted by movement on my left. Scanning the branches of the nearby trees, I saw a small brown bird rustling about. He fluttered and jumped and then, when finally free of the branches, flew off. I turned to my right and recalled that, somewhere amid the tall grass, there was once an old farm site where, in the early decades of the twentieth century, the air was filled with the lively sounds and sights of the Bill Lynch carnival. For a time, I pictured the Haligonians who made their way across the harbour's mouth to this field in a temporary escape from the grinding thrum of the city. Still, the pressing silence and eerie stillness gave such imaginings an ominous quality, like an unspoken tragedy that hung over a halted conversation.

I felt the same unease about the telephone poles that came in regular intervals on the trail. The poles suggested something of the settlement that once gave this island life. Yet, still strung with sagging black wires, the poles seemed long past their prime, gently leaning this way and that, slowly succumbing to rot and decay. Walking farther along, I recalled that somewhere to my right lay the crumbling, mossy foundations of an old schoolhouse and the remains of the McNab's Island lighthouse.

After a time, the rocky path became thick with grass, and the trees on both sides gave way to a wide stretch of green ferns. It was then that I was aware of having wandered onto a cut grass lawn. As I passed by a narrow thicket of pine trees to my right, a light yellow, two-storey house with green trim came into view. My tourist map informed me that this was the Mathew Lynch house, a grand home built in the early 1930s. Though I knew the house was empty, and had been for many years, I felt awkward as I strolled casually across the yard, past a broad, covered porch overlooking a long stretch of grass, still mostly green. Somehow, I expected the screen door to open and someone to yell, "What the hell are you doin' in my yard!"

So I hurriedly left the Lynch house property and immediately came to the backside of another home, a three-storey, white and red trim affair called the Davis-Conrad house, built in 1917. The green of the trees in the backyard gave the scene a late summer feel. Again, I somehow expected to see life here, perhaps a child running through the yard kicking a ball. Yet, as I passed closer to the house, I noted the signs of long decay – chipped paint and weathered wood, a property well past the point of easy repair.

Just due west of the Davis-Conrad house sat another home, a light blue bungalow, which, according to my map, housed the island's caretaker. Even here, where I knew someone lived, the house and the yard surrounding it seemed unnervingly silent and still. This feeling was amplified as I turned away from the house and came upon an old red Suzuki SUV parked crookedly on the grassy lane. The inspection sticker on the car indicated that it had been on the island for more than a decade, though how long it had actually been sitting at the side of the road was unclear. As with the houses, the state of the car gave me the eerie impression that it had been hastily abandoned, as though some terrible event had occurred and the driver escaped, running in fear from the scene. As I casually examined the car, I reached around to the side pocket of my bag and removed a water bottle. I opened it and took a long drink. Turning to lean against the car, my thoughts returned to the sick and dying passengers on the S.S. *England*.

"It was very cold on the journey," remembered Henry Wenner. The illness that overtook the passengers, he noted, "began with dysentery, cramps, sharp pains in the side, the eyes became large and the feet icy cold." The rate at which the sick succumbed varied. "Some were sick for four days," Wenner recalled. "Others were well in the evening and in the morning, a corpse." Soon afterward, Wenner was personally struck by the tragedy. "Our party of six also lost one of our members, Jacob Sontag, who was stricken the day before we were shipped to [McNab's] island."

For a time, I considered the victims of that first night. In particular, I thought of the eight-year-old German boy and wondered about the wrenching fear he must have felt and wondered about his mother who had held him so tightly as he called for her. Then I thought about the bacteria that killed him.

The cholera or Asiatic Cholera that infected the young boy was a microscopic organism that looked vaguely like a miniature sausage with a tail. In small numbers, the bacteria were harmless. However, once the bacteria found their way into the warm, moist confines of the human intestines, they began to reproduce at an extraordinary rate. And as they reproduced, they created a thick, mucousy layer in the small intestine, which produced toxins that were absorbed into the intestinal cells. These toxins, in turn, upset the capacity of the body to maintain an appropriate water balance. The infected body, confused by this imbalance, began expelling the body's fluids – in some cases up to thirty percent of a human's total water in a matter of hours – through vomiting and diarrhea. The characteristic diarrhea of the cholera was described as having a "rice water" appearance, which in reality indicated the rich habitation of the bacteria. Often this "rice water" found its way into other water sources, where it waited to invade the next host.

Ironically, the cholera bacteria were not the killers of the host – dehydration was. Having expelled so much fluid, the victim lost much volume of blood. This lower blood volume caused the blood to become thicker, which in turn caused the heart to pump faster in an effort to ensure the body's vital organs – in particular, the brain and the kidneys – continued to operate. As this occurred, non-vital organs began shutting down, and blood was restricted from flowing to the extremities, causing a pricking or tingling sensation. Soon afterward, an insatiable thirst developed. The victim felt stomach pains, muscle cramps, or muscle spasms followed by the rapid evacuation of the bowels.

Terrifyingly, the patient was keenly aware of his or her experience. Yet, when the heart failed to sustain blood pressure, the patient grew lightheaded and often passed out. Meantime, the body continued its expulsion of fluids; the victim's pulse increasingly became faint; a dark blue hue crept over the skin; the eyes began to sink into sockets; the lips became dark blue; and the nails became livid. As the body began losing its fight, the kidneys would fail. Bodily waste then quickly accumulated in the blood, and finally, when it could sustain the stress no longer, the heart simply gave out and stopped.

This was how the young German boy died in the arms of his mother.

The image of the dead boy in his mother's arms stayed with me as I walked away from the abandoned homes and the red Suzuki SUV parked askew on the trail. I ambled farther along Old Military Road in the near silence, the only sound at my feet where some fallen leaves crunched gently under my step, until I reached the iron-gated entrance to Fort Ives.

The spot was named for New Englander Benjamin Ives, who had spent time in Louisbourg on Cape Breton Island in 1745 when the British were in possession and later came to Halifax when it was first founded. The fort itself was built in the decade between 1864 and 1874. Today, the site was little more than a deteriorating collection of stone and brick fortifications.

I casually entered the compound and strolled onto the wide grassy centre where low, windowless brick buildings spread themselves in a seemingly random pattern. To my immediate right, resting on a row of long wooden blocks, were six rusting, ten-inch muzzle-loading cannons. I walked past these to a set of granite stairs, at the top of which was another cannon, resting on a retractable steel carriage. The cannon's muzzle still pointed at what was once an opening in a stone and metal encasement but was now a cavity filled with earth and weeds. I clambered atop the encasement and took in the view.

The sights from here were striking. I spent some minutes letting my eyes follow the horizon, looking from Halifax to the Eastern Passage shore. Then I clambered back down into the fort, and for a time I playfully poked around, looking inside each of the dank and empty stone buildings. I was conscious that, in 1866, as the ill-fated *England* sailed toward Halifax, this fort was lively with a construction crew. I imagined their presence here in those hours before the arrival of the ship and imagined something of their day-to-day labours and their mundane worries.

After wandering about for a while, I found a spot on the grass at the base of a nondescript, squared stone building and sat. Rummaging through my bag, I found a banana and a granola bar, and while I ate, I let my thoughts wander aimlessly from the past to the present and back again. Finally, when I finished my snack, I again returned to my bag and removed a series of papers, mostly copies of *The Halifax Citizen*, and reviewed the local news for April 3, 1866. In particular, I looked for an article entitled "Curious Theory of A Canadian Physician."

"Dr. J.A. Crevier of St. Cesaire, Lower Canada," read the article, "claims to have discovered the true nature of the Asiatic Cholera, from microscopic observations taken in 1849, and in 1854, upon a number of patients. [The doctor claims] he has found the disease to be animalcular, produced in the stomach and the bowels by an immense quantity of small animals, which he classifies as Infusory Zoophytes of the Vibronian Family, and Bacterian genus. They can be carried about a long distance either in the system or in clothes and breed rapidly where ever there is filth, and animal or vegetable matter in a state of decomposition. Thus, a miasmic poisoning is produced, and may be introduced into the arterial blood, through the breathing of the lungs.

"Choleric symptoms are only the healthy effort of the system to rid itself from the poisonous animalculae, through intestinal exudation. True remedies are only such as help that effort of the system, the best medicine being that kills the animalculae, without injuring the digestive organs.

"The value of the above plausible theory depends upon the correctness of the microscopic observations of Dr. Crevier, about which, however, he is very positive, having seen, he says, the animal alive, and observed it also when killed by medicaments. Others have also used the microscope in time of cholera, without being able to reach safe conclusions."

I was struck by the coincidence of this article in the paper, appearing just days before the arrival of the S.S *England*. The decade-old resistance to the compelling theory of contagion in favour of the Miasma Theory was puzzling to me. In 1854, as James Glaisher studied the dense blue mist for the General Board of Health of London, British scientist Dr. John Snow had isolated the London cholera epidemic to a single well in the Soho section of the city, proving that cholera was indeed a water-borne disease. And though Snow himself did not quite reach the point of arguing in favour of contagious microscopic bacteria, Crevier's article clearly indicated that the idea was floating in the scientific air.

Yet I wondered if perhaps this resistance to Contagion Theory was literally bred in the bone. After all, what was more powerful than fear induced by smell? Removed as we are from the nineteenth century, I wondered if we had simply lost touch with the powerful smells that inhabited the times. With no refrigeration and with poor sanitary conditions, any city of the age would have been pungent to say the least. "If a late twentieth-century person were suddenly to find himself in a tavern or house of the period," wrote Dickens's biographer Peter Ackroyd about the city of London, "he would be literally sick – sick with the smells, sick with the food, sick with the atmosphere around him." This natural aversion to smells would have been a powerful check to any logical supposition that illness might be caused by something unseen or microscopic. Ironically, the Miasma Theory induced sanitary reforms that kept the bacterial cholera contained, thereby reinforcing a belief in the false theory.

Having finished the article, I gathered my bag, and with my thoughts still drifting through blue mist miasmas and multiplying bacteria, I left Fort Ives and travelled along a trail called Forsythe Street. The grass of the street quickly returned to a rock- and mud-filled lane flanked by thick groves of spruce and elm. After a time, I passed a grey cement block of a building on my right, which my map informed me housed the Department of National Defense electronic listening station. Deteriorating dismally as only cement can, the cracked and chipped building was besieged by the creeping green foliage of the forest. After looking over the site, I left the electronic listening station and plunged deeper down the path, returning my thoughts to the S.S. *England* and the events in Halifax.

On Thursday, April 5, 1866, William Rose, aged fifty-six, died after a long illness, "leaving a wife and six children to mourn their loss." The widow Elizabeth Wilson also died in her sixty-first year, while a "short, severe illness" took the life of Hanorah Gaul, thirty-four, "the beloved wife of William Gual, leaving a husband and three children to mourn her loss." At the same time, a "revolt in the Provincial Penitentiary was promptly suppressed by the firmness of the Governor, Mr. McGregor, aided by sergeant's guard from the tower at the fort."

Over the Friday and Saturday, April 6 and 7, 1866, Margaret, "wife of Edward Kavanagh, aged fifty-eight years," passed on, her funeral to be held in "her late residence, Maynard Street, on Sunday at two o'clock." Friends and acquaintances were asked to "please attend without further notice." John Patrick, aged one year, seven months, and ten days, the "second son of Elizabeth and James O'Connell," also died, as did "Harriett, only daughter of William McDowal, Jr., of this city, aged twenty-one years, after a lingering illness."

With the Fenian threat still a concern, the *Citizen* reported that a "Second Brigade of Militia Artillery" was formed "under the command of Major W.H. Creighton," as well as a Naval Brigade, "of which B. Wier, Esq., is to be Lieut. Colonel, and D.H. Pitts Major." The paper announced, "We are glad to see an organization so necessary to our coast defense thus started, and we trust its formation will be speedy and successful."

As well, "on Saturday afternoon, between three and four o'clock, as the schooner *Gilbert Bent* was leaving this port, a young man named Robert Hatfield, aged twenty-eight years, accidentally fell overboard and was drowned. Every effort was immediately made to save him, but it was impossible as there was a heavy sea on and the boat instantly filled when lowered. The schooner returned to port."

In Pictou, Nova Scotia, the *Citizen* reported that "the storm of Friday last, caused considerable damage in various parts of the country. The immense chimney connected with Mr. Logan's Tannery, three-mile house, was blown down during the gale, and crushed in the roof of his bark-house. A barn belonging to Mr. Desmond, and a building belonging to Mr. Meager were also blown down; and others were more or less injured. The dwelling-house now being erected by Mr. Abraham McDonald, near Campbell's Tannery, was wrestled from its foundation, and materially injured by the violence of the wind. Shingles, in very many instances, were torn from the roofs and scattered to the winds; fences were leveled; and many fine trees were broken and uprooted. Between forty and fifty telegraph poles were dislocated between Truro and Pictou alone." Similarly, "during the terrible storm ... a barn belonging to Mr. Angus McDonald was blown down at the South River. A barn at the North Grant, belonging to Mr. John McDonald, was also blown down by the same gale."

In Lawrencetown, Jacob Durlino told his neighbours, "Having had the misfortune to have my dwelling house consumed by fire on the 26th, and a large part of its contents, my neighbours repaired to the forest, cut, hewed and framed a building, and erected it on its base in the very brief space of two and a half days."

In the Halifax courts, James Lawlor was deemed drunk but excused. Patrick Haley, "lying drunk in the street was sentenced to pay the cost of trucking him to the station." Ann Morash was "charged for deserting her child, and remanded for examination." Edward Neary, "who escaped from the Poor House, was sent back to that institution." At the same time, Ann Wilson was "sentenced to six months in the city prison as a common vagabond, while Reuben Cross, a marine of H.M.S. *Rosario* convicted of being drunk was sent on board his ship." And "several boys, charged with having disturbed the public peace on the Sabbath Day, were remanded." Finally, on Saturday, April 7, 1866, the city was horrified to hear the tale of a boy who, while "wandering over the North Common on Tuesday morning, found the dead body of a female infant packed in a wooden box."

On board the S.S. *England*, the deaths continued, leaving Captain Grace and his crew overwhelmed. When members of his crew finally fell ill, Captain Grace realized that New York was too far away for help. He ordered the ship to change its course and headed to the nearest port – Halifax, Nova Scotia. "Finding it impossible to reach her port of destination," remembered Ambrose Martin, "the steamer was headed for Halifax, which port she made on the night of April 8. We hurried on to Halifax. We arrived there during the night. Next morning, early, our dear and sorrowing commandant hoisted the yellow flag, and signaled to the shore for help."

Henry Wenner also remembered the change in destination. "We sailed until the 8th of April," he wrote in his letter to his parents, "when we arrived in Halifax. Here the cholera raged fiercest. There was much sorrow, weeping, and wailing."

As I imagined the weeping and wailing, Findlay's Cove opened up to my right and Forsythe Street again reconnected with Garrison Road. The grey clouds still hung overhead, and the wind still came in sharp gusts. After a time, I came into sight of McNab's Cove, where I scanned the waters, now choppy with the wind. When I reached the north side of Government Wharf, I again imagined the *England*, arriving in the gloom of night on April 8, and saw her anchor about fifty yards from me.

"For four nights previous," remembered Reverend Martin, "I had not closed my eyes. This fatal night, while going on my rounds with the doctor and searching every berth, picking up the departed, we met with three of the sick writhing in agony." Amid the gusting wind, I could still hear the weeping and wailing and hear the strange juxtaposed sound of hammers on wood. "During the night of our arrival," recalled Martin, "there was not a breath of air. [Only] the frequent blows of the hammers used in making coffins alone broke the silence." This was Henry Wenner's memory as well. "She came to quarantine," said Henry, "and all night long the silence of the calm night was broken by the sounds made in making coffins."

In his memoirs, the Premier of Nova Scotia, Dr. Charles Tupper, also recalled this day, though he misremembered the date. "On the 10th of April," he wrote, "the ship *England*, bound to New York, which had sailed from Liverpool on the 25th of March with 1,200 passengers beside the crew, put into Halifax in distress. One hundred and fifty-six cases of Asiatic cholera and fifty-six deaths had occurred. The dead bodies were towed in boats behind the ship, and the pilot brought her into the quarantine station on McNab's Island."

Tragically, the pilot who brought the S.S. *England* into the harbour also contracted the illness. "A pilot, with an assistant and his son," remembered one Halifax resident, "went off to the ship in an open boat. Hearing that there was sickness on board, the men remained in the boat, which was towed at a considerable distance astern by a ten-fathom rope. In this way the ship, with the boat in tow, was conducted to her place of anchor. The pilots then went on shore, and were never on board the infected ship. In the course of the next two days both men were seized with cholera, and one died. Both men communicated the disease to their families. In the family of one there were three cases, but no death; in that of the other, besides the father, who died, there were four cases and two deaths. The only other cases of cholera at Halifax at that time occurred in the family of a man whose two children were seized after playing with some soiled bedding which had floated on shore from the infected steamer; one child died, the other recovered. The mother also took the disease, and died. Surely if disease was ever communicated by infection it was so in the case of these three families, the different members of which were in various ways brought into contact with the infecting material imported by the steamer."

Enveloped by an imaginary darkness, I pictured the grim scene of that night. "On our deck coffins were piled up," said Reverend Martin, "and when permission was given to bury our dead we lowered four boat-loads, and, in the presence of our affrighted passengers, we slowly wended our way to the shore to give as good and Christian a burial as we could."

In my mind's eye, I watched the boats being rowed to shore, imagined the bodies being unloaded and laid, side by side, on the beach. Then, one by one, the bodies were carried into the woods. I turned and watched as the bodies were gently placed on the ground, amid the shadows and trees, and then listened to the living dig the shallow graves of damp earth for the dead.

With this imagined scene playing out in my mind, I looked away from the forest and began walking south along Garrison Road. As I did, McNab's Cove gave way to glimpses of the rocky Mauger's Beach and the Lighthouse Road, which gave way to the dark, marshy stretch of McNab's Pond. Before me, curving off into the shadowy wilderness, lay the narrow path.

Somewhere there, hundreds of desperate emigrants camped among the trees in fear of their lives.

5

Mustard Poultices

"MUSTARD POULTICES – These should be applied to the pit of the stomach, and kept on till the surface is well reddened. The patient, however well he may feel, should observe perfect rest. To lie quietly on the back is one-half the battle. In that position the enemy fires over you, but the moment you rise, you are hit. When the attack comes in the form of diarrhea these directions will enable every one to meet it successfully. But when the attack is more violent, and there is vomiting, or vomiting and purging, perhaps also cramps and colic pains, the following mixture is far more effective, and should always be resorted to. The missionaries Messrs. Long, Throwbridge, and Washburn have used this in very many cases and with wonderful success.

"It consists of equal parts laudanum, tincture of capsicum, tincture of ginger, and tincture of cardamom seeds. Doses, 30 to 40 drops, or half a teaspoonful in a little water, and to be increased according to the urgency of the case. In case the first dose should be ejected, the second, which should stand ready, should be given immediately after the spasm of vomiting has

ceased. During this last cholera siege no one of us failed of controlling the vomiting and also the purging by, at most, the third dose. We have, however, invariably made use of large mustard poultices of strong pure mustard, applied to the stomach, bowels, calves of the legs, feet, etc., as the case seemed to require."
– Dr. Cyrus Hamlin, Constantinople, 1865

*F*rom McNab's Cove, Garrison Road crossed the narrow centre of the island and then wandered through a tight grouping of trees and past more greying telephone poles that marked the distance along the path. I sauntered along a lazy, left-hand curve on the same stretch of road that had brought me up from Wreck Cove, until I came upon another fork. I gamely took the narrow trail to the right, which arced pleasingly through a stretch of yellow grass climbing steep embankments along both sides. I considered that the unique banked design of the path was likely crafted with some defensive protection in mind as the road slipped furtively into Fort McNab.

In addition to Fort Ives, Fort McNab was the only other significant fortress on the island. Of course, at the time of the death ship's arrival in Halifax Harbour, this area was little more than a compound for the McNab family, which included a modest family cemetery, my intended destination. With some sense of irony, I considered that the cemetery was the only real evidence that the McNab family had ever lived on the island. But the side path to the graveyard had grown so thick with foliage that I missed it and instead found myself amid the crumbling brick, stone, and cement of Fort McNab.

The fortress had been built between 1888 and 1892 and was regularly occupied by the military until the early Cold War, finally being decommissioned in 1959. The spot held a commanding view of the harbour's entrance and, as such, was designed to be a fearsome gun battery and gatekeeper to the harbour. That said, the fortress was, in reality, little more than an oval-shaped road dug into the top of a drumlin. Basic encampments, storage facilities, and gun batteries had been built along the banks that hugged the road. Most of these reflected a World War Two refit, amounting to a thin coating of cement over Victorian era constructions. As I walked into the fortress grounds, I could still see the stone and brick arches of the older buildings where the cement had crumbled away. Here, unlike Fort Ives, the grass had grown wild and tall. As I poked my head into the dank, doorless rooms that faced onto the path, I imagined the place humming with Victorian era soldiers, trying to keep warm on a chill evening.

Wandering slowly around the Fort McNab buildings, I reached a wide cement staircase that lead to a gun battery. Carefully, I climbed the broken stairs, where grass and weeds grew up from the cracks, to the wide gun platform above. The old gun had been removed long ago, leaving behind the iron, semi-circle track on which it would rotate. At the waist-high cement wall, I threw my leg over the lip and pulled myself up. Standing on the ridge, I took in a deep breath and looked back into the fortress, where cement peeked out from thick under-brush. Then I turned to my left and viewed the mouth of the harbour and the open Atlantic ocean, which rippled rich white and dark blue under the grey, cloudy sky. To my right, in the distance, I caught glimpses of the Halifax skyline and its wharf-filled waterfront. Looking toward the north end of the island, I surveyed the lighthouse at the end of Lighthouse Road and then turned my attention to McNab's Cove. For what seemed a long while, I imagined the S.S. *England* anchored there late on April 8 and early on April 9, and then imagined life in the city just before the citizens became aware of the ship's arrival.

On Monday, April 9, 1866, William Connors, "a native of County Waterford, Ireland," passed away at fifty-nine years of age, while the Rev. Archbishop Gray died at aged sixty. Not far from Halifax, Jeramiah Gerror died at age thirty-seven after

suffering "a short illness of inflammation." He left "a discon-
solate widow and six helpless children to mourn the loss of
an affectionate father." In the Halifax courts, "William Miller
and Samuel MacDonnell," both members of the provincial legislature, pleaded "guilty to a charge of having assaulted A. J.
Richie, Esq., proprietor of the *Sun* newspaper, in the street."
William was fined $20 and Samuel $10.

The provincial government offered a $100 reward "for the
capture of four deserters from the 16th Regiment, who recently
committed a highway robbery at Porter's Lake, near Dartmouth." Also, the papers reported that "a schooner arrived
here on Sunday from Portland, with a cargo of material for the
street railway. This work is being pushed forward with all possible speed, and the line is expected to go into operation about
the first of May." At sea, the "ship *Cordelia Morris*, at Boston
from Newcastle, Eng., reported, [that a sailor was] lost overboard, a Mr. Miller, seaman, of Newport, NS, aged nineteen."

Meantime, in McNab's Cove, as dawn reached over the
island, an emergency yellow flag was raised above the deck
of the S.S. *England*. Among the first to respond and arrive
from Halifax was the shipping agent of the Cunard Shipping
Lines, Mr. James Morrow. Morrow was a capable and quick-
thinking man, who carefully assessed the seriousness of the
situation. With Captain Grace, he discussed the possibility of
providing a doctor for the ship to continue south to New York
City. But Captain Grace knew the cholera outbreak among his
crew made this impossible. His crew was sick and exhausted,
he explained. Too many had contracted cholera. In addition,
more than forty bodies had already been buried at sea over
the last two days and the passengers below were dying by the
dozens. The crew members not sick were kept in near constant
motion, crafting makeshift coffins and burying the dead. "The
deck," observed Reverend Martin that morning, "was heaped in
coffins."

Morrow promptly sent a report of the crisis to the city health officer, requesting permission for the ship to anchor off McNab's Island. He then prepared for the healthy passengers to disembark from the ship onto the island and for the dead to be buried. "Permission having been given," noted Reverend Martin, "four boatloads of coffined emigrants were conveyed to the island where they were buried. The steamer was ordered to anchor at Meagher's Beach."

James Morrow also made the request for another ship that might be used as a floating hospital. In response, an old hulk, the *Pyramus*, anchored in the Navy Yard was offered. The *Pyramus* was "an old teak Danish-built, first-class 28-gun frigate, that was captured with seven others by Nelson at the Battle of Copenhagen [in 1801]." The ship, having been "fitted with jury masts and sent to England" for a time, was then remanded to Halifax, Nova Scotia, in 1833 or so. For decades she sat strangely juxtaposed against the modern vessels in the Halifax Navy Yard, acting as a floating hospital for invalid sailors in port and as temporary accommodations for sailors displaced when their vessels underwent refit. Broad and spacious, the *Pyramus*, or "the hulk," was perfect for Morrow's task and was promptly towed to the island. Morrow then returned to the small skiff that had brought him to the island and rowed to the city, where he gathered volunteers.

Still standing atop the gun battery in Fort McNab, I removed from my bag a photograph of the *Pyramus*, taken in 1870, while she sat in the Halifax Navy Yard. The picture was taken in winter, the road in the foreground white with snow. The ship sat at the dock on the left with the Navy Yard buildings sprawling off to the right. Scrutinizing the photograph, I noted that the wide-hulled ship, with its eighteenth-century gun ports and stylized aft windows, looked strangely out of place in the context of a mid-Victorian-era shipyard with long, low brick buildings of pitched roofs and small narrow chimneys. The *Pyramus* by then had been stripped of her masts and appeared, in the picture, more like a floating residence or store-house.

I looked up from the picture and glanced back at the Halifax skyline. As I did, I thought about the events there as James Morrow arrived back in the city to pass information and gather volunteers. Already, word of mouth had spread the news of the death ship in Halifax Harbour. Among those preparing to leave for the S.S. *England* was the city's health officer, Dr. John Slayter. On that morning of April 9, his features no doubt betrayed a seriousness of purpose as he kissed his wife and children goodbye.

This grim scene was in stark contrast to the evening of April 7, 1866, just two days before. On that night, an excited Dr. John Slayter arrived home on Argyle Street, just four blocks up from the waterfront. At thirty-six, Dr. Slayter was in the prime of his life and in the flower of his career. He was a prominent citizen – a well-respected doctor and now the City Health Officer. He was also a member of a successful family with a long history in Halifax. He was the great-grandchild of another John Slayter, an original settler of Halifax, who had been among those occupying the French fortress of Louisbourg in 1745. That John Slayter, with his wife Jane Allen, moved to the new settlement of Halifax in 1749 and quickly became one of the prominent merchants of the young city. His son and grandson both followed him as prominent merchants and nota-ble citizens.

Clearly, fate had smiled on John Theordore Harding Slay-ter, born in Halifax on April 7, 1830. His was a life of com-fort and privilege – of good schools, good homes, and a good future. As a young man, studious and ambitious, he travelled to New York City, where he studied medicine, returning to Halifax upon graduation, a newly minted doctor, and set up his practice. Not long after, he met Mary Robinson, daughter of Joseph Robinson, Esquire. They fell in love and married in late 1857 or early 1858. Their first son, Joseph, was born in

1859. Their second son, John, was born in 1861, followed by William in 1863 and Frank in 1865. And while his family grew, so too did John's practice and his place in the community. By the time Frank was born, Dr. John Slayter had already been appointed Health Officer for the port of Halifax.

As he arrived home on April 7, 1866, John Slayter was likely greeted by his four boys and Mary, now two months pregnant with their fifth child. And no doubt the mood was festive since this was John's thirty-sixth birthday. Of course, what John and his family did that evening is lost to history. Still, I imagined that there was a gathering of friends arranged by Mary. A fine meal was served around a well-set table. Likely, there was talk of the city, and later, perhaps over wine or port, talk of the Fenian threat or the politics of Confederation. And perhaps, as the evening wore on, and the guests finally departed, John took stock of his life, as so many do on their birthdays. Certainly, had he done this, he would have felt a fine sense of success, professionally and personally. And he would have had good reason to believe that continued success would follow.

History does not record how Dr. John Slayter received the news from James Morrow's messenger, early on April 9, though it would be safe to say that the letter arrived at Dr. Slayter's home. I imagined the messenger racing up the four blocks from the waterfront and through the streets at dawn. And although the facts delivered to Dr. Slayter were scant, they must have been sufficient to paint a dire picture. Dr. Slayter would have understood the gravity of the situation and quickly gave the messenger his orders for how the S.S. *England* was to be handled: the ship was to be anchored off Mauger's Beach and not allowed near the city.

Then, from his desk, Dr. Slayter took a small sheet of blue, lined paper and crafted a note to Dr. Charles Tupper, Premier of Nova Scotia and Provincial Secretary. "Halifax NS. April 9th/66. Hon Provincial Secretary," wrote Slayter in a spidery script of thin black ink. "I beg to report the arrival of the Steamship *England* – [Captain] Grace Master – from Liverpool, Great Britain, with 1202 passengers. On Tuesday last, a case of cholera appeared. Since then there have been 160 cases and 46 deaths. At present there are on the sick list 30 patients. Fresh cases are appearing. I have secured the ship off the lighthouse." Slayter finished the letter, "Your obedient servant, John Slayter, Health Officer." When the ink dried, Dr. Slayter folded the note twice and handed it to the messenger for immediate delivery.

News of the death ship in Halifax Harbour travelled not just through the city during those first hours but also around the globe. *The New York Times* received and published four successive dispatches through Monday, April 9, 1866. The first dispatch reported, "The steamship *England*, from Liverpool March 28, via Queenstown 29th, arrived this morning [at Halifax] for medical aid. She now lies below the lighthouse." Soon after, at 11:30 a.m., the second dispatch was made: "The agent of The Associated Press has thus far been unable to board the steamship *England*, no communication being yet allowed between her and the shore. Every effort will be made to obtain her news."

An hour later, at 12:30, the *Times* released its third dispatch: "It is reported that the steamship *England* has the cholera on board. She has been sent to the lower quarantine. The Agent of The Associated Press is still endeavouring to obtain her news. The *England* has 1,200 passengers." Finally, the fourth dispatch of the day read, "The steamship *England*, which arrived here from Liverpool this morning, had one hundred and sixty cases of cholera on board. There were forty deaths during the passage."

Back at his home on Argyle Street, Dr. Slayter gathered his medical kit and other supplies. He embraced his sons and bade his wife goodbye. In haste, he then headed for the waterfront, where he boarded a skiff with other volunteers and headed across the harbour's mouth to the anchored S.S. *England*.

Upon arriving, he climbed the ladder to the deck and found a scene of terrible desperation. He navigated between the coffins until reaching Captain Grace, who greeted him formally. After a brief exchange, Dr. Slayter was shown below deck. What he found there was equally horrible. In the dim light, Dr. Slayter was overwhelmed by the smells and sounds of the sickness. As his eyes adjusted to the darkness, he became aware of the myriad bodies huddled in bunks and on the floor. So, too, he began to take stock of the many dying and dead "in their bunks, while others were huddled in the odd corner, breathing their last."

Immediately, Dr. Slayter ordered that the dead be removed. The volunteers who had accompanied him to the island and the exhausted crew carried the bodies onto the deck. Once there, "short iron bars were attached to the feet" and the bodies were heaved overboard. They sank quickly into the dark water of the cove. According to a later account, "fifty to sixty" bodies were "thrown overboard that night."

Before climbing off the Fort McNab gun battery wall, I took one last look at McNab's Cove. The wind, blowing in gusts, had created long ripples along the surface of the water, and the grey clouds overhead now suggested the possibility of rain. As I watched, I imagined the stricken ship that first night and listened to the slap of the bodies against the water as they dropped, one by one, into the cove. I also imagined those on deck watching the grim business of securing short iron bars to the feet of bodies. For a fleeting moment, I even imagined the scene beneath the cove's surface, with the bodies moving like strange weeds, drifting gently this way and that with the movements of the murky water.

After a deep breath, and a long sigh, I clambered down the wall and then descended the cement stairs to the grassy path below, where I wound my way, counter-clockwise, about the fortress road until I returned again to my point of entrance. There, walking along this narrow road, I searched for the hidden path to the McNab family cemetery. Yet, even with a concentrated effort, I almost missed it again. After some backtracking, I finally came upon the trail and worked my way along until I came to the small cemetery, enclosed by a tall, chain-link fence.

The scene was modestly unsettling. Even before the chain-link fence was added some years ago, author Thomas H. Raddall described the cemetery as "the world's best defended graveyard." And, indeed, given its distance from the city, and given the fortress and fence that enveloped it, the graveyard was truly well-guarded. The headstones that I could see appeared in reasonably good shape, in better shape than much of Fort McNab. And the lettering on the faces of the stone markers was distinct and legible, even from the distance of the fence.

Though I couldn't quite locate the stone, I knew that the bones of Peter McNab lay somewhere here. Peter had purchased much of the island from members of the Cornwallis family, relatives of the founder of Halifax, on Christmas day in 1782. Later, he purchased additional land from Joshua Mauger, making Peter the island's sole owner. His son Peter McNab II later left much of the island to his oldest son James. After some time as a merchant on the island, James McNab went into provincial politics. In an effort to raise money to support his political career, he began selling off parcels of land in the 1840s. His younger brother, Peter McNab III, also inherited a large part of the island from his father, about 120 acres. After Peter III's death in 1856, his wife also began selling off portions of the island. All the while, the McNab family members were interred in this small space from 1809 until 1863, although according to my guidebook, the last family addition to the plot was Ellen McNab, who passed away in 1934.

With my fingers loosely grasping the chain-link fence, I scanned the stones, reading what I could about Mary Ann and Edwin, Charles and Peter, Ellen and Joanna. As well, I noted the headstones of married relations – Hugonin, Roderick, James, and even some others whose stones I found difficult to read. Scanning the grounds, I noticed in the corner, amid the stones and the tall grass, the tops of two small wooden crosses. From what I could tell, these crosses were without names and, according to my guidebook, remain something of a mystery. Some have speculated that they marked additional unnamed McNab family members. Others believed they sat atop the graves of soldiers who were stationed at Fort Ives. Yet, perhaps most intriguing, still others have surmised that the rotting white crosses, hiding amid the tall grass and stones, might well be the gravesites of S.S. *England* cholera victims. So, for a time, I let my mind return to the scene playing out on the death ship.

Even as Dr. Slayter boarded the *England*, in the late morning of April 9, 1866, he knew that, given the nature of such diseases, a place for burial of the dead, away from the living, was immediately required. He decided on a location far from the island's settlements, at the far southern end of the island, called Thrumcap. Thrumcap was a secluded, heavily wooded, uninhabited area attached to the main body of McNab's Island by a natural rocky causeway, though some confusion remains today as to whether Slayter was referencing this part of the island or a smaller island just to the west called Little Thrumcap.

Still, either site could only be reached by boat, rowing from the *England* past the lighthouse and across open water, which could quickly become choppy. But before burials here could be attended to, Dr. Slayter began the challenging work of separating the sick from the healthy. This took much of the day. Later, as the daylight began to wane, the dark scene became more dismal as a mixture of snow and rain began to fall. Amid this scene, Dr. Slayter organized the bodies for burial on Thrumcap then spent the remainder of the night attending to the sick and dying. When dawn returned, he set out with volunteers to bury the dead. It was after he returned to McNab's Cove and the S.S. *England* later that morning that he wrote another letter to the Provincial Secretary, Charles Tupper, on a long sheet of white paper.

"April 10th/66," Slayter began. "The Honourable The Provincial Secretary. Sir, I proceeded to McNab's Island this morning with a working party to dig graves and have chosen Thrumcap the extreme southern point as the most desirable place. There are 18 dead bodies at present and the disease has spread rapidly. There are now from 150 to 200 cases. In fact, fresh cases every hour.

"I have had about 400 removed to the *Pyramus* and will have the rest encamped if the *Pyramus* is over crowded. I will remove more of them ashore. It would be desirable for the preservation of life to have a place at once for the recuperation of the sick. They must be kept warm and as cases accumulate remove them at once from non-infected cases. The only way ... is to obtain the [residence] vacated today by the officers. It is empty and I think can be obtained from the general. As I have had to go on board the *England*, I must put myself in quarantine. Besides, the doctors are completely worn out. I have written for [Dr. John] Garvie and [Dr. Charles] Gossip so as to give them a chance of organizing themselves. I wish to put one in the *Pyramus* and the other in camp. The boundary arrangements had better be attended to by Dr. [W.N.] Wickwire and if help is required by Dr. Pryor or any other you wish to appoint. If any ship with sickness comes in, I will attend to them.

"I should like a boat to come near the ship every day so as to communicate out for anything required, a police force had better be sent down – other men if possible. I will take care as communication occurs and after command from the ship I can report the disease with accuracy. I have not the slightest doubt if the emigrant agent would come on board, he would find lots of settlers ready to leave at once. I have the honour of being your obedient servant, Dr. Slayter, Health Officer."

Once Slayter finished writing his letter, he folded it and handed it to a boatman, who set off toward Findlay's Wharf and a waiting skiff. Slayter then returned his attentions to the sick passengers on board the *Pyramus*, which now sat anchored to the stern of the *England*. At the same time, Slayter oversaw the transfer of healthy passengers to the island, where tents were now being erected, each with a wooden floor and straw bedding. All the while, the heavy, wet snow and rain continued to fall. To keep warm, emigrants and volunteers began cutting down trees and setting alight great fires. I imagined the emigrants huddled around the blazes, with blankets supplied by the Cunard Lines hanging loosely over their shoulders.

"We are informed that a large number of blankets and other necessities were put on board the *Pyramus* this morning after which she was towed down to the quarantine station by the Cunard Steamer *Merlin*," read the *Citizen* on April 10. "It is reported that some 30 coffins have been sent on board the *England*, in order to have the dead buried as quickly as possible. Twelve deaths are said to have occurred on board since she arrived in port."

At the same hour, *The New York Times* reported that "Capt. Grace, of the steamship *England* [said] that on Tuesday the first case of cholera occurred, since which time one hundred and sixty more cases have broken out, and fifty deaths have occurred. She was ordered off by the Government. But owing to the rapid spread of the disease, and the engineer's being sick, it was found impossible to proceed. She now lies [north of] the lighthouse. Part of the passengers will be placed on board the hospital ship, and shanties erected on the beach for the sick. There will be no communication with the ship. The authorities are doing all in their power to relieve the unfortunate passengers. There are three doctors on board to look after the sick. She has 1,202 passengers, and 100 crew. The passengers are principally German and Irish. The Captain thinks the disease was brought on board by the German passengers."

"Now cleared of our dead," Reverend Martin later wrote, "we hurried our healthy passengers to McNab's Island, close by. Tents were soon erected, beds and bedding were placed at the disposition of those who wished to take them, abundance of clean, fresh straw was provided, and everything was made as comfortable as possible. Six doctors from Halifax generously hastened to our relief, and having our own ship's doctors, Mr. McCulloch, Dr. Heath, Dr. Albert Voelges, and Dr. Richard Thomas, the services of these gentlemen were put in immediate requisition."

Back in Halifax, the morning newspapers had gathered all the fragments of news available and reported to the citizens. The headline of the *Citizen* for Tuesday, April 10, 1866, was nothing short of alarming. "CHOLERA," the paper's headline read in bold letters. "Advance Guard of the Plague – Three Horrible Invaders – Cholera, Small Pox, and Typhoid Fever in One Emigrant Vessel!

"The S.S. *England*, Capt. Grace, 12 days from Liverpool bound to New York, with 1,202 passengers and 100 crew, put into this port yesterday for medical assistance. The captain reports that Tuesday last a case of cholera appeared, and since that time there have been 149 cases of sickness on board, out of which number 49 died, and 69 are now on the sick list. We are also informed that five deaths have occurred since her arrival here. Three separate forms of disease are reported to have broken out among the unfortunate passengers, viz: Cholera, Small Pox, and Typhoid Fever, and from the large number who have fallen victims, these must have appeared in their most virulent form.

"It being reported that medical aid was needed, Dr. Garvie of this city offered his services to go in the ship to New York, and render any assistance required. This offer was accepted by the authorities; but the captain stated that he was unable to proceed, on account of the sickness of his engineers. This looks like an excuse, as the engineers who brought her in were probably able to take her out again. We are informed that under these circumstances permission has been granted by the authorities to transfer to the receiving ship *Pyramus*, as many of the passengers who have not yet become infected, as she will accommodate, and land the remainder on Meagher's beach, where tents will be provided to shelter them.

"The sick are to remain on board until they become convalescent. Most of the passengers are German and Irish emigrants, and it is supposed the cholera was brought on board by the former. It may seem hard to send a ship on with so many passengers in such a condition; but it may also be a question, which would be the more humane course, to order her to proceed on her voyage or that she should be allowed to remain and land her passengers here, where there is no proper hospital accommodations, and when the quarantine station is in such close proximity to the city, that the danger to which the inhabitants of the whole Province are exposed, is frightful to contemplate.

"Notwithstanding the large amount of talking which has been done in the City Council, and the numerous warnings that have been given through the press and in other ways, not a step has yet been taken to improve the sanitary condition of the city, and if Halifax should now be visited with cholera, we fear that it would be found exceedingly difficult to control the ravages.

"The *England* will probably not be the only visitor of this description that we shall have this season. Every plague-stricken ship crossing the Atlantic, will strive to make the nearest port after disease makes its appearance on board. Steamers are now leaving the other side of the Atlantic from Liverpool, Glasgow, Bremen and Havre, at the rate of nearly one a day, most of them crowded with passengers, and it is vain to hope that these ships will all escape the fate of the one that entered our port yesterday. With the approach of warm weather the cholera must be expected to appear among their passengers under the most careful management; and cases as in the present, now that the precedent has been set, that Halifax will be used as an outwork of defence to protect the cities of the United States from the plague.

"The arrival of the vessel should compel the health authorities to treat this matter as a grave and pressing emergency; and not an hour should be lost in enforcing the strictest sanitary regulations, and in taking every step that providence can dictate to prevent the spread of contagion."

Surveying the white crosses in the McNab family cemetery, I thought about the wave of fear that must have overtaken Halifax by April 10. Cholera had visited before in 1832, and hundreds had died. Though the city had been spared from the cholera epidemic of the mid-1850s, the earlier epidemic was still within living memory. Those walking the streets in 1866 would have looked with growing suspicion at dark puddles that filled the rutted, earthen roads.

Throughout the day on April 10, 1866, on the island and onboard the S.S. *England* and *Pyramus*, Cunard agent James Morrow worked desperately amid the chaos. Deeply concerned about the situation, he stole a few minutes away from the seemingly endless work late in the afternoon to write a note to Dr. Tupper.

"My dear Sir," he began. "From tidings I get tonight I think it highly desirable to send another doctor to the *England*. The Captain sends me word. His staff members are exhausted and so are his crew members. I am trying to get some men to go down tomorrow to assist generally, but especially, to clean the ship. The report is more favourable and things generally look brighter, but entre nous, there is some great bungling about the burial of the dead. The Captain writes me they are not buried yet. That was at six p.m. tonight, and some of them died yesterday. I fear Slayter is so busy with the living he has had no time to attend to the dead. I sent men this morning a flat for the coffins. They have come back and report the gear's ready. I think you had better get [Police Chief] Jarvice or whoever else goes.

"I am especially [concerned about attending] to the burial of the dead immediately on arrival at the ship. I do not understand why this very important matter has been long delayed but it is now a very important matter indeed and must be attended to at once. Probably Slayter has it in mind and only needs time to attend to [it. One of] the men who came back with me [said] that while they were digging, a coffin floated ashore with a body in it and they placed it in [a] pit. The captain says the boat with the dead is still astern (3/4 miles distant). You can quite understand the need of action. I am quite done out or could come down myself and see you. Yours Truly, James D. Morrow."

If Tupper responded to Morrow's concerns, the letter has been lost.

Meantime, an exhausted Dr. Slayter wrote Charles Tupper for the second time on April 10. "*England* 1866," he began. "[To the] Hon. the Provincial Secretary. Sir, not one man ashore has taken the disease. [They are each] in splendid condition, and I feel certain they will continue. So I want to send more on shore from the *Pyramus*. I have sent for tents. I have good reason for encamping them where they are, but my hands are too sore at present to work much, and I want to send off letters at once for … the mortality on board is very bad. I think upwards of 40 died within 12 hours. There are about 100 on the boat at present. I would keep this quiet.

"There is not the slightest danger of the disease being communicated into town. I will also give my reasons for believing so. The cholera is of the worst description. The preliminary symptoms [come quickly] and death [comes] in a few hours. After morning, I took 20 or 30 dead bodies around to Thrumcap for burial, a precarious time. We had no one who would assist. Garvie, Gossip, and Frank Garvie are acting well and up to the mark." He finished the letter, "I have the honour to be yours, Dr. Slayter, Health Officer."

Below his signature, he added a postscript. "Emigrants from Ship *England* to be cleared back from Ive's point beyond the isthmus at [Mauger's] beach, searching all houses on the island north of that point. A line to be provided out and marked by pickets on the isthmus, confining all emigrants to the south side of the island, with orders to warn and shoot any persons passing to the north of that line. Tents to be pitched on the green hill, and no one allowed in Captain Lyttleton's barn or premises."

Standing by the McNab family cemetery, I took one last look at the weathered white crosses, allowing that perhaps they were indeed markers for the S.S. *England*'s dead. Then I let go of the chain-link fence, turned away, and descended the path that led out of the McNab family compound and headed through the fortress entrance. At Garrison Road, I glanced left, then I turned right and headed south with some vague notion of finding the ground on which, according to Slayter's letter of April 10, the emigrants were to have camped.

6

Collapse

"COLLAPSE – This is simply a more advanced stage of the disease. It indicates the gradual failing of all the powers of life. At a certain point the body of the patient begins to omit a peculiar odor, which I call the death odor, for when that has become decided and unmistakable I have never known the patient to recover. I have repeatedly worked upon such cases for hours, with no permanent results. But the blue color, the cold extremities, the deeply sunken eye, the vanishing pulse are not signs that the case is hopeless. Scores of such cases in the recent epidemic have recovered. In addition to the second mixture, brandy (a tablespoonful every half hour), bottles of hot water surrounding the patient, especially the extremities, sinapisms and friction will often in an hour or two work wonders."
– Dr. Cyrus Hamlin, Constantinople, 1865

I walked south along Garrison Road until I was presented with another fork. Referencing my map, I noted that the trail to the left was a continuation of Garrison Road, which curved still farther left and then descended a modest slope back to Wreck Cove. The path to the right was called Culliton Farm Trail, and it ran south along the high ground of Range Hill, down through a spongy marsh, and then up again to Green Hill at the far south end of the island.

Since Green Hill was my intended destination, I opted to take Culliton Farm Trail and happily ambled on. That said, just a few dozen metres down the path, I found still another fork to consider. As with Culliton Farm Trail, the alternate path, called Rifle Range Trail, ran along the high ground and south to the marsh at the foot of Green Hill, in an almost parallel track to Culliton Farm Trail. I looked back to the fork at Garrison Road and Culliton Farm Trail and took some note of the surroundings with a vague idea of remembering a marker to avoid getting lost. I mentally noted a crooked elm, pointing north on Garrison Road, and turned back, assessing the two trails. With each path looking decidedly narrow and wet, I shrugged and headed south along Rifle Range Trail.

After a few minutes of trudging through soft ground and wet grass, I came upon a series of concrete platforms partly hidden in the bushes to my right. These oddly shaped forms constituted two 800-yard rifle ranges, one for sailors and one for soldiers who were often encamped on the island. If there had been any targets 800 yards down the way, they were long gone, and the range area itself was well along in the process of nature's repatriation. Looking at the platforms, I considered that they were much like the other cement structures I had seen on the island, seriously deteriorated with long weeds and gnarled branches literally growing up and through the myriad cracks and chinks.

Leaving the rifle range, I continued down the trail, thinking vaguely about the deteriorating platforms. I found myself oddly conscious of having left behind the north end of the island, with its wider roads and family homes, its brick fortresses and family cemeteries. In fact, I was struck by how quickly the wilderness had reached with growing confidence into the faint path before me and how much those human-made structures had given me the comforting illusion of civilization.

Walking farther still into the forest, I felt the wind pick up again, blowing in gusts through the leaves. In front of me, the lane curved gently left, and then right, before settling into a long straightaway that ran through the unseasonably rich green of the ferns and trees. Despite my efforts to stay on dry ground, it wasn't long before my shoes repeatedly sank into the wet, spongy grass. And as I quietly grumbled, I wondered if hikers regularly trekked this way, or if they trekked this way at all. Of course, given my search, this terrain somehow seemed appropriate. After all, it was here, on April 11, 1866 – amid the shadows of these woods, with the snow and rain falling – that the tenuous light of civilization flickered in the face of fear. With this in mind, I stepped off the path and perched myself on the trunk of a felled tree. After taking a drink of water, I reached into my bag and removed more papers from the red folder and reviewed the goings-on in Halifax.

On April 9, *The Halifax Citizen* reported that Florence Elizabeth died "of consumption, after a long and painful illness." She was, the paper noted, the "daughter of Mrs. Hannah Barker, deeply mourned by her sorrowing relatives and friends." On April 10, Mr. Edward Robinson died at sixty-six years of a "disease of the heart." On April 11, Wallace, the "infant son of Thomas and Lavinia Reyno," died at the age of just ten months of causes unsaid, while "at Brookside, Prospect Road … after a lingering illness, Thomas Stone, a native of Weymouth, England, [died at] aged 76 years, an old and respectable inhabitant of that place."

In the shipping news, I read of "the ship *General Williams*, of Yarmouth, [under Captain] Hatfield, from Liverpool to Boston." The ship "was abandoned on the 13th February, [the] crew taken off by the S.S. *Darien*, and hence to Barbados." On the "18th, eight men were transferred to the *Thornton*, from Liverpool to New York, which put into Fayal [in the Azores] on the 7th March, with loss of rudder." As well, the schooner *Cornucopia*, which "arrived at Boston on the 5th inst, from Barbados [on the] 10th, reports that previous to sailing a steamer arrived, having on board Capt Hatfield and crew of ship *Gen Williams*, from Liverpool Dec 25th, abandoned in a sinking condition. [The ship] was set on fire before the crew left [it]."

In the local courts, "Samuel McDonnell, MPP, was charged with an assault on Mr. J.H. Stewart, convicted and fined $20 or 20 days County Jail. Mr. McDonnell was also bound over to keep the peace for six months. Benjamin Bailey, for assaulting Laughlin McPherson, who is dangerously ill, remanded until to-morrow." Mary Murphy was "charged with begging on the street, admonished and dismissed," while James Hogan, "taking Thomas O'Brien's cab without permission," was also "admonished and dismissed." Reuben Ashton, of HMS *Duncan*, was found to be "drunk [and] ordered to be sent on board his ship." Sarah York – "coloured," notes the paper – was "charged with an assault on Sarah Skinner" – "whitey-brown" it read – and was "dismissed." Finally, "a complaint [was] … made by Alderman Roche and Mr. Wm. McKay against W.D. O'Brien, Esq., of the City Railroad Co., for creating a nuisance on the street by scraping the mud to the sides and allowing it to remain … A fine of $1 was imposed."

Under the title "CITY INTELLIGENCE," the *Citizen* also reported on the S.S. *England*. "A fishermen rowing his skiff up the harbour yesterday," it reported, "came in contact with something in the water, which on examination proved to be a coffin containing a dead body, supposed from the steamship *England*. It would thus seem that the officers of that ship avoid the trouble of burying their dead by quietly slipping the coffin over the vessel's side into the water of the harbour, where they may drift out to sea, or up to the vicinity of the town, as the winds and tides may chance to carry them. The attention of the city authorities was called to the circumstance, and we presume that steps have been taken to prevent contagion from being floated into the city in this manner. A report from the Medical gentlemen on board this unfortunate ship, gives the information that among the passengers who have been removed to the shore, no new cases of the disease had occurred.

"Among those already infected, the deaths during the past two days have averaged from eighteen to twenty. It is now generally understood that the disease is not cholera, as was first supposed, but an aggravated form of ship fever, probably induced by the crowded state of the vessel and the battening down of the hatches in heavy weather. We may add that the rumour current this morning, of the death of one of the Medical gentlemen from the city is entirely without foundation. We are happy to state that letters received from these gentlemen this morning report them all in perfectly good health."

As I looked through the newspaper clippings and letters, I thought about the passengers. Some, terrified by the mounting deaths and deteriorating situation amid the makeshift tent camps, made a rash escape into the woods, running south along the path where I now sat. I imagined their confused state as they ran, their heavy breathing, their desperate searching for something that would give them cause for calm. Some of these emigrants ran until they fell against a tree or collapsed in the snow, realizing, in their exhaustion, that they too had cholera. I imagined the horrors of their final hours, lying in the woods alone, their bodies convulsing with the loss of fluids, their hearts pounding with fright. I imagined them facing their fear, resignation, and death.

At midday on April 10, 1866, a skiff moved steadily across the mouth of the harbour. On board sat Drs. Charles Gossip and John Garvie, as well as John's younger brother, Frank, who was home from his medical studies at Harvard. When Frank had heard that his brother was heading to the island, he eagerly volunteered. No doubt they sat silently while the boat was rowed steadily toward the island. After arriving at Findlay's Wharf, the three joined Dr. John Slayter. They spent that first evening separating the sick from the well on board the S.S *England*, then moving those with symptoms to the *Pyramus* while moving the others to the island. By all accounts, their work was performed amid the near chaos of wandering emigrants and volunteers.

During the first few days, they found little time for sleep, and when dawn arrived on April 11, the doctors made their way to the wharf where two boatloads of bodies waited for transport to Thrumcap. With so few willing to take on the dangers of this work, Dr. Slayter himself had prepared the bodies, loading them into the boats. Yet, before he left for Thrumcap, he received his first correspondence from Dr. Charles Tupper.

"Wednesday, Provincial Secretary's Office, Halifax 11th April 1866," Tupper began. "Sir, I have it in command from His Excellency the Lieutenant Governor to direct you to cause the immediate removal of everything connected with the steamship *England* to Green Hill near Thrum-Cap and to prevent any communication between the ship or any one connected with any other portion of McNab's Island.

"His Worship the Mayor is now sending a police force who will be instructed to act under your direction. All the dead bodies must be buried at Thrum-Cap in deep graves as soon as possible after death. There is a narrow neck of land between Green Hill and the other portion of the island, which is to be so guarded as to prevent any communication with the quarantine station. A vessel in which the police force will live could be used to secure communications.

"I am further instructed to ask you to make detailed reports of the character and content of disease up to the present time, and a daily report subsequently for the information of the government. Thanks," concluded the letter with surprising informality, "Dr. Charles Tupper."

Born in Amherst, Nova Scotia, in 1821, Charles Tupper was the son of a stern Baptist minister. As a child, he attended school in Wolfville, Nova Scotia, and later travelled to Edinburgh, Scotland, to study medicine. After earning his medical degree, he returned to Amherst in 1843 and opened a practice. A dozen years later, in 1855, Tupper entered politics, running for the Conservative party in the Cumberland riding against the well-known and popular Joseph Howe. To the surprise of many, Tupper won that race and began a spectacular career in politics. Moving to Halifax in 1859, Tupper quickly engaged energetically in politics while at the same time setting up a medical practice. In 1860, he became Provincial Secretary.

"When we returned to power in 1863, I had obtained a medical practice so large and lucrative that I could not afford to abandon it," remembered Dr. Tupper. "I formed a co-partnership with Dr. [William Nathan] Wickwire, and remained in the practice of my profession. I at this time held the positions of leader of the Government (which involved the leadership of the House of Assembly), and City Medical Officer, which I did not resign until during the session of 1866, when I had carried the measure for the organization of the Halifax Hospital and Poor Asylum. In addition to these duties I wrote almost all the political leaders [editorials] in the *British Colonist* when in Halifax from 1855 to 1870." On May 11, 1864, Tupper became the Premier of Nova Scotia.

In his April 11 letter to Slayter, Tupper was firm in his instructions. As a doctor, Tupper understood – in what would be considered progressive for the time – the great risks of contagion, which was the reason for his insistence on the Thrumcap burials. The desire to move the emigrants was likely a result of pressure to protect the others on the island from contagion – Colonel Westmacott's men, for instance, who were stationed at Fort Ives in addition to the year-round residents.

Indeed, the effort to relocate the emigrants was already under-way.

Westmacott's commander, Hastings Doyle, had already received instructions from the Lieutenant Governor, Sir William Fenwick Williams. From my red folder I retrieved a copy of the letter Doyle sent to Williams.

"Head Quarters, Halifax NS, 12th April 1866," Doyle began on a sheet of unlined, blue, loose-leaf paper. "To His Excellency, The Lieutenant Governor of Nova Scotia. Sir, In compliance with the orders contained in your letter of this day's date, I have the honour to acquaint your Excellency that I have given directions for a party of 2/17th Regiment to be held in immediate readiness to proceed to McNab's Island. I request to be favoured with Your Excellency's instructions as to the nature of the Duty this detachment is to be called upon to perform and to what part of the island the emigrants now in Quarantine are to be confined and as it will probably be necessary to use force to fire upon those who will not obey the law, whether a magistrate will be in attendance, to accompany the troops on all occasions which is absolutely necessary. I beg to state I am not aware of the laws relating to Quarantine and shall be glad, should any exist to be favoured with a copy of them – I have the honour to be your obedient servant, Hastings Doyle, Major Feneral Command."

Among the emigrants, Henry, Mary, and Margaret Wenner, still without symptoms of the illness, had been removed from the S.S. *England* to the island. In his letter to his parents, Henry recounted that, after two days on the boat, surrounded by the sick and dying, "we were placed on the island on April 11," where he and his sisters were given a tent with a wooden board floor and fresh hay. The De Jong and the Healy families, too, were moved to the island and into tents. Aris Eelman and

Klass Vlaming were not as fortunate. Both contracted cholera and had been moved to the *Pyramus*.

Meanwhile, the Hardens were deemed well enough to move to the island. There, Harry Harden took charge and watched over his brothers. Having served with distinction in India, he also stepped forward and volunteered. When Dr. Slayter asked if he would assist in the burial of the dead, Harry agreed without hesitation. As for the other emigrants during those first few days, hundreds were moved to the island, where they milled about uncomfortably on the beach and on the hill just above the water. Remembers one volunteer from Halifax, "They suffered much from the cold."

Among the saloon passengers, matters were somewhat different. Though they too were moved to the island, the disease affected few. "Not one of the saloon passengers," wrote Dr. Tupper, "was attacked." Although this was not entirely true, the relatively few cases of cholera among the saloon passengers suggests that they were kept away from the third-class passengers for the duration of the quarantine. That said, saloon passenger Reverend Ambrose Martin answered the call of his profession and laboured greatly among the ill, dying, and dead. After the first night in the habour, he had helped to bring emigrants to shore.

The chaotic work continued unabated through the day and into the night of April 11. There was no rest. Dr. Slayter spent much of that time rowing to Thrumcap, where he dragged coffins from the rocky beach and into the woods. There, he and his volunteers dug the burial pits and interred the dead through the day and into the night. When dawn had again reached across the island on April 12, Dr. Slayter took a few minutes from his work and composed another letter to Tupper.

"Steamship *England*. April 12th 1866," began Slayter's letter. "Sir, In reply to your communication of Saturday I beg respectfully to state that owing to the lack of means of transportation at my disposal and the unruly conduct of the passengers your instructions relative to the sick cannot be carried out as fully as I could wish. The recent prevalence of high winds and the nature of the beach rendered impossible to land the infected persons at the Light House whilst to have kept them on the steamer would not only have infected all on board but would have generated a pestilent atmosphere which would have endangered the city.

"By prompt separation of the sick from the well and isolation of all from the ship the disease is rapidly being checked, and the great change leads me to hope that there is not the slightest contagion where cleanliness can be enforced and fresh air procured. Since the removal of the healthy portion of the passengers from the ship no fresh cases have occurred with the exception of some ... who had evidently been previously infected. I regret to state that on the hulk *Pyramus*, which I have converted into a hospital ship the contrary has been the case. The average mortality is about 25 per day. Last night 15 died. And there are now between 50 and 60 cases on the list.

"With regard to the burial of the dead on account of the scarcity of coffins, and great obstacles I have to contend with in having graves dug of a proper distance, some few were thrown overboard heavily weighted ... In reference to perfect isolation I would recommend that a cordon of volunteers be drawn round the woods occupied by the passengers. Would you kindly suggest this? The Guard Ship detailed for duty has arrived and will doubtless prove of material assistance to me. In conclusion I will take every opportunity in my providing [letters] making your acquaintance with the progress of the disease. I have the honour to be your obedient servant, Dr. Slayter, Health Officer."

Once completed, the letter was promptly sent to Tupper, who upon its receipt responded in kind late that same morning. "Sir," Tupper wrote to Slayter on April 12, "I get to acknowledge your letter of today informing me that you had not sufficient force to give effort to the commands of His Excellency the Lieutenant Governor respecting the due observance of Quarantine and to inform you that His Excellency in Council has been pleased to appoint you a Justice of the Peace for the County of Halifax and has obtained a military force to proceed to your aid under your directions in enforcing the quarantine regulations. You are hereby instructed to swear in the police force, which has been sent to the island, and a special constable to act in conjunction with the military. I am further instructed today that His Excellency relies upon your carrying into effect the instructions previously given and taking every precaution in preventing the escape of any persons from the quarantine, any improper communications with the ship or Hulk or anything being done to endanger the Health of the Community. I have the honour of being your servant, Charles Tupper."

As I finished reading the letter, I shifted my position on the tree trunk and folded the papers in half, slipping them back into my bag. Then I pulled out my water bottle and took another long drink. For a time, I thought about the events of those three days.

When I finished the water, I glanced to the path and noticed, lightly grooved into the grass and mud, what appeared to be the footprint of an animal – two small oval shapes, side-by-side, about three inches long. Although I made no claim to know about such things, a quick referencing of my guidebook told me that these marks almost certainly belonged to a white-tailed deer. According to the book, the island apparently supported a modest herd of them, a dozen or so, which swam regularly between Eastern Passage, Lawlor's Island, and McNab's Island.

Admittedly, the deer print unnerved me, not because of an unusual phobia of deer, but because it reminded me that I was sharing the island with a variety of other creatures. According to my reading, my island mates included the Maritime garter snake, the northern redbelly snake, the Eastern American toad, the northern spring peeper, and the eastern redback salamander – not one of which, to my knowledge and relief, was either large or poisonous.

Among my feathered island friends at this time of year were chickadees and nuthatches, crows and jays, sparrows and finches, a European starling and a cedar waxwing, grosbeaks and flycatchers, and a basic winter wren. So, too, there were blackbirds and warblers, thrushes and woodpeckers, loons and grebes, cormorants and great blue herons, gulls and ducks and geese. And finally, there were the eagles and falcons, ospreys and hawks, and even the odd owl that called this island home from time to time.

Among my mammalian island mates were the red-masked shrew, the little brown bat, the northern long-eared bat, the American red squirrel, the meadow jumping mouse, the mink, and the snowshoe hare – though according to those who keep track of such things, the snowshoe hare had not been seen, officially at least, on the island for many years.

Mind you, none of these animals gave me much cause for concern. Nor did I fret much about the reports of a single beaver that was said to have resided on the island for a brief time in the late 1990s. Apparently, that beaver had built a spacious dam near McNab's Pond where – being something of a romantic and despite, one assumes, a courageous effort to find a mate – the poor flat-tailed fellow remained steadfastly alone. After a season or two on the island, this lonely beaver waddled away from his dam and swam off to look elsewhere for love.

No, the love-starved beaver did not worry me. But what did give me a modest amount of anxiety – sitting alone, in the middle of the forest, in the middle of the harbour's mouth – were the notably larger and more dangerous animals that were said to roam these woods. In the late summer or early autumn of 1991, for instance, a lumbering, berry-mad black bear created some lively and confused moments when he happened on a peaceable hiker. Fortunately for both the bear and the hiker, they were sufficiently startled by each other's presence that a good distance was made between them before the breathless hiker found his way to the authorities. Of the bear nothing more was heard.

If this was not enough to give the solitary hiker on McNab's cause for concern, the black bear sighting occurred at about the same time as another animal sighting – that of a large, and most likely randy, bull moose. Again, I could only imagine the face of the startled hiker who blithely turned the corner on the south end of the island to find himself face to snout with a large, cud-chewing moose enjoying his late morning victuals. No doubt the moose was modestly bemused at the sight of the hiker turning sharply on his heels and racing headlong into the forest. Even though neither bear nor moose had been sighted on the island since, I found myself giving the woods around me a long, nervous inspection.

Foolishly, I re-referenced my guidebook in some vague effort to allay my fears by confirming that these sightings were just one-time events. But I discovered to my horror that I had, in fact, even more to worry about. Although no official sighting on the island had ever been reported, it appeared – according to those who spend their time searching for such things – that, found in the woods around me, were prodigious amounts of coyote scat. Worse still, there were those who fervently believed – though one hopes just for the sake of bragging rights – that it was reasonable to assume that the island might support the odd bobcat. Wide-eyed, I shut my guidebook and stared uneasily into the trees, repressing images of a rabid bobcat mauling.

No doubt my rising anxiety was augmented by my attention to the dark tale of a death ship and the idea that decomposing bodies, rife with cholera, once lay in the grass not far from where I sat. Clearly, the blue mists were getting to me. I decided it was better to be on the move than to sit still, so I stood and gathered my things. For a moment, I glanced north and then turned south, heading deeper into the wild toward Green Hill and Thrumcap.

7

Thirst

"THIRST – In these and in all advanced cases, thirst creates intense suffering. The sufferer craves water, and as sure as he gratifies the craving the worst symptoms return, and he falls victim to the transient gratification. The only safe way is to have a faithful friend or attendant who will not heed his entreaties. The suffering may be, however, safely alleviated and rendered endurable. Frequent gargling the throat and washing out the mouth will bring some relief. A spoonful of gum-arable water or chamomile tea may frequently be given to wet the throat. Sydenham's White Decoction may also be given, both as a beverage and nourishment in small quantities, frequently. In a day or two the suffering from thirst will cease. In a large majority it has not been intense for more than twenty-four hours."
— Dr. Cyrus Hamlin, Constantinople, 1865

Archeological evidence suggests that humans may have first passed through McNab's Island some 10,000 years ago, not so long, geologically speaking, after the vast Wisconsin ice sheet of the last ice age began to recede. This same evidence also suggests that these first ancient humans were nomadic hunters, travelling east from what later became New Brunswick, and north from what is now New England. Likely they travelled in small family groupings in pursuit of caribou herds that journeyed across land bridges submerged long ago in the North Atlantic.

In their many seasonal camps along the way – including Nova Scotia sites in faraway Debert and nearby Lake Micmac, Harlten Point, Dartmouth, and on McNab's Island itself – these mysterious early humans of North America left behind various hand-fashioned tool kits of small, stone arrowheads and hand-sized scraping rocks, the arrowheads for hunting and the scraping tools for skinning the caribou and cutting the fish and waterfowl. As well, archeologists found in later nomads' camps stone axes, adzes, and gouges.

As the seasons, years, and centuries passed, such human settlements became regular features of the area. The local successors to these mysterious first peoples called themselves Mi'Kmaq, and according to tradition and archeological studies, they were known to have spent their summers on the Dartmouth shores opposite McNab's Island, hunting and fishing, leaving behind their prehistoric garbage piles in the form of shell middens. Whether or not these people, or the mysterious nomads that preceded them, ever stayed for extended stretches on McNab's is open to debate. That said, if they had set up camp, it would have been for the warm months only, since the harsh winters would have made year-round habitation difficult.

I found myself thinking about these early people as I walked along the trail, the closeness of the trees and the thickness of the brush, combined with the ever-narrowing path, giving me a sense of stepping back through the ages. Here, sound was so faint and spare at times that my eardrums seemed to push out, reaching with some desperation for the organized rhythms of civilization. Despite the nearness of Halifax, my growing sense of isolation was now wholly consuming.

Marching with something of a determined cadence, I passed an inviting path to my left, which cut east to Culliton Farm Trail. A few dozen yards farther along, I walked by another, more defined, path called Searchlight Road, which worked its way west, down to the water's edge. I was tempted to turn here, particularly given the increasing muddiness of Rifle Range Trail, so I stopped for a moment and scanned the trail's viability. I was hoping to find a way to Thrumcap, where so many of the cholera victims had been buried, and I considered the beach as a means to get there. But for long stretches, the shoreline offered difficult terrain with jagged rocks and rolling stones. Obviously, a straight muddy path, though modestly uncomfortable, would be far less troublesome. So I turned away from Searchlight Road and continued determinedly south along Rifle Range Trail. As I walked, I thought about the beach and of the first Europeans who arrived at McNab's Island.

Those first Europeans, arriving in the last years of the seventeenth century, were French fishermen who used the shores to build fishing stations for drying their rich catches of cod. They named this island Isle de Chibouquetou, a French spelling of the Mi'Kmaq name, what the English would later call Chebucto. For a time, I imagined the tough circumstances of these French fishermen's lives, imagined the rough-hewn houses in which they slept and ate when not working in their boats or on the beach.

Sharing the island with these rough fishermen and the nomadic Mi'Kmaq were Catholic missionaries. One missionary in particular, about whom we have some knowledge, was a fellow named Father Louis Peter Thury. Thury was born around 1644 in Normandy, France, where he studied to become a priest. After turning thirty years of age, and having finished his studies, he was sent to Quebec where he was ordained as a priest on December 21, 1677, and worked among the settlers. Six years after that, in 1684, Thury, who must have shown interest in missionary work, was sent to live among the Mi'Kmaq in Shubenacadie and Chebucto. His efforts were clearly successful, for four years after, Thury was sent to Penobscot, in what would later be the state of Maine, to work among the natives. Reportedly, his success there was such that he was again summoned to Nova Scotia in 1696, where he made Chebucto his home not long after the French fishermen had staked their claims on the island's shore. We know that Thury stayed long enough among the Mi'Kmaq to die there in his fifty-sixth year on June 5, 1699.

What scant knowledge we have of Father Thury's life among the Mi'Kmaq comes from another Frenchman, a surgeon and amateur botanist named Diereville, who sailed into Halifax Harbour in October of 1699. Diereville carefully recorded his adventures and described Isle de Chibouquetou and the fishing station that was erected on the beach. "[The building was] half as long and quite as wide as the Mall in Paris," Diereville wrote, "built on a fine beach along the River [the harbour's mouth] and at a distance which permitted the water to pass under it at high tide and carry away the refuse of the cod." By the time Diereville had arrived at Isle de Chibouquetou, the French fishing station had already been abandoned as unprofitable.

As Diereville observed the station that day, he noted in his journal that a group of Mi'Kmaq approached the ship in "little bark canoes." After a formal greeting, the Mi'Kmaq encouraged Diereville and his companions to visit the island. So they did. After arriving on the beach, Dereville recorded that the Mi'Kmaq seemed friendly enough, though he did notice, with perhaps a raised eyebrow, that they were "armed with musket and hatchet."

On the island, the group gathered to eat. "I gave them a good breakfast of meat and fish and they munched biscuit with the best appetite in the world and," he noted somewhat anxiously, perhaps glancing again at the muskets and hatchets, "[they] drank brandy with relish and [in] less moderation than we do." As they ate, Dereville noticed "on sitting down to table, they [the Mi'Kmaq] said their prayers devoutly and made the sign of the cross and when they had finished, they gave thanks with the same piety. Each had a Rosary around their neck." Such observations suggest that Father Thury was reasonably successful, from the standpoint of the Catholic Church at any rate, in making the rituals of Catholicism attractive to the Mi'Kmaq.

Perhaps pleased with the opportunity to explore the local geography, Diereville stayed among the Mi'Kmaq for a few days more, hiking, eating, and drinking. And before he left for France, Diereville was taken by the Mi'Kmaq on a journey into the woods – to a place not far, perhaps, from where I now walked – and shown Father Thury's grave. It was, Diereville recorded, little more than "a tomb of stakes, covered with bark." Though this firsthand description of the Mi'Kmaq and Father Thury was brief, it stands out as the first written observations of life on McNab's Island. I thought about these details, my mind filling with images of dilapidated fishing stations and rough encampments, of men carrying muskets and hatchets and drinking too much brandy. So, too, as I pushed farther into the woods, I imagined the grave of Father Thury.

It occurred to me, as I walked, that this whole area – McNab's Island, Halifax, Dartmouth, and Eastern Passage – might well have remained lightly inhabited had it not been for its attractive harbour. During the eighteenth century, the see-sawing ownership between the French and English of the grand fortress Louisbourg forced the English to find and build a new settlement to protect its interests in New England. As a result, Halifax was founded on the eastern side of a large drumlin that faced the harbour island, which at the time was given the name Cornwallis Island, in honour of the settlement's founder, Edward Cornwallis.

Soon after the founding, Cornwallis Island became a place for ships to replenish supplies, for cattle to roam undisturbed, and for trees to be felled, floated, and used for fuel in Halifax. In 1752, Governor Cornwallis bequeathed the island to his nephews Henry, James, and William. Locals grumbled about this. Said one about Cornwallis's land grant to family members, "[H]e gave to his family the very best island in the harbour of Chebucto, called Cornwallis Island, which in my opinion should be given in small farms to the many settlers of Halifax, instead of cooping them up on a small isthmus." It certainly didn't help matters that Henry, James, and William never resided on the island. Still the Cornwallis family maintained business connections there for more than three decades, until they put the island up for sale in 1772 for the princely sum of £1,000 sterling. The price must have been dear. There were no takers until Peter McNab laid down the money in December of 1782.

I continued walking, feeling claustrophobic in the thick forest, though occasionally meandering amid modest stretches of tall grass and felled trees. When traversing through these open areas, I often caught glimpses in the distance of the Atlantic Ocean. But such clearings were small and quickly enough I found myself enveloped again by the forest.

After travelling through what seemed an endless wilderness, I noted that the path had become distressingly faint. In fact, more than once I was convinced that I had lost my way among the trees. I gave some thought to turning back, but followed what I assumed was the path around a sharp bend, where it abruptly stopped at a four-foot drop to a narrow canal of rust-red water running west to east. Facing me on the opposite side of the canal ran a six- or seven-foot cracked cement wall that sprouted a spider's web of rusted iron rods and angled brackets. The surreal image amid the wild of the forest was disconcerting. For a time, I looked at the construction and tried to make sense of the works, putting the pieces together into some recognizable whole. But an intelligible design eluded me. Clearly, something had been built here. That much was certain. But I hadn't any sense of what it might have been. Adding to my confusion, my guidebook suggested nothing human-made existed past the rifle range platforms.

Thoroughly perplexed by this industrial age art piece – and without a path on which to travel – I scanned the woods around me until I spotted another fallen tree on which to sit. So I sat. When I was settled, I reached into my bag for a map, hoping to find another means to Thrumcap. While removing it, I also removed my red folder, which I lay beside me on the trunk. After scanning the island map, I realized with some disappointment that, short of trudging through the pathless forest, I would likely have to make my way to the water and then labouriously south along the beach. Knowing how rocky the beach could get, I was uncertain as to my plan of action, so I did nothing. Instead, I turned to the red folder, removed some papers, and reviewed the goings-on in Halifax in mid-April of 1866.

On April 13 and 14, 1866, the *Citizen* reported that "on Saturday morning, Matthew James, son of Patrick Mahony, [died] in the 24th year of his age." The funeral was arranged for "Monday, at half-past three o'clock, from his Father's residence, No 9 Bishop Street." All "friends and acquaintances [were] respectfully invited to attend." As well, "after a short illness, Edmund, youngest son of Patrick and Ellen Power," died at the age of "15 years and 6 months." His funeral was arranged for the following "Sunday, at two o'clock, from his father's house, 73 Park Street." So, too, "after a short illness, Thomas Michael, eldest son of Patrick and Catherine Donohoe, [died] in the "17th year of his age." Funeral services would also occur "Sunday next, at 2 o'clock, from his father's residence, 49 Maynard Street. Friends and acquaintances [were] respectfully requested to attend."

"Jason Kent, Esq, [died at] aged 82 years." He was "an old and respected resident of Musquodoboit," and left "a large circle of relatives and friends to mourn their loss. His end was peace." Nova Scotian Richard Hill, youngest son of Charles J. Hill, died "at Batavia, Island of Java, on the 18th January last, in his 31st year," while "Mary Jane Finigan died in New York." She was "the beloved wife of Mr. George Finigan, and second daughter of Mr. Archibald Lyon of this city." She was thirty-five years old, and left behind "a husband and 5 children to mourn her loss."

Also passed away was "John Evan, the beloved son of Evan and Isabella Campbell, aged 7 years, 4 months and 19 days," and "suddenly, this morning, William Henry, son of the late Henry Scott, [passed] in the 30th year of his age. The funeral will take place on Monday next at 3 o'clock from his late residence, 29 Falkland Street. Friends of the family are requested to attend without further notice." Finally, Charles Henry Thedweil Symonds died at aged 33 years. His funeral would occur at his "late residence, No. 2 Creighton Street, on Monday, at 4 o'clock, p.m. Friends of the family are invited to attend."

In the local courts, John McKay and Henry Shaw were charged with being intoxicated. John was excused, while Henry "a man of war sailor," was "fined $2 for being drunk in the streets." Julia Kelly, "an old offender," was again "found drunk" and "sentenced to 90 days in the city prison under the vagrancy act." Elizabeth Carroll, "found wandering in the streets in company with a soldier, was sentenced to one year in the City Reformatory," while William Murphy and Margaret Howard were also charged with being drunk. William was "excused" while Margaret was "sentenced to 20 days city prison." Also found drunk was Charles Allen, "sentenced to 20 days city prison," George Saddler, "admonished and dismissed," and William Boyle, "a seaman of H.M.S. *Duncan*," who was "ordered to be sent on board his ship." Jane Plank and Thomas Wier were also charged with being "drunk." Jane was "discharged on taking the pledge," while Thomas was "fined $1 or 10 days city prison." Edward Shehan was charged with being "drunk and assaulting his father," for which he was "sentenced to 90 days city prison." And Robert Joint was "charged with fighting on the street." He was "convicted of being a common vagabond and sentenced to 90 days city prison."

The paper also reported, "[A] sad occurrence took place to-day resulting in the death of Mr. [W.H.] Scott, book-keeper in Mr. B. O'Neil's establishment. Between 10 and 11 a.m., Mrs. Scott heard a report of firearms in her bedroom, and proceeding thither found her husband prostrate on the floor, with a pistol shot wound in his head, from the effects of which he died about an hour afterwards. A great many contradictory reports are in circulation about the distressing event, but there is reason to believe that the fatal shot was fired accidentally. An inquest will be held this evening. Mr. Scott was an estimable young man, and leaves a widow and three children."

So, too, the paper reported on the S.S. *England*. "The passengers on board the steamer *England*," reported the paper alarmingly, "are allowed to throw overboard their cast-away clothing, the consequence of which is, that portions of it have floated up towards the city, and washed ashore at the south-end. [At the same time,] a detachment of the City Police have been detailed for duty at the Eastern Passage to prevent the *England*'s passengers from wandering over McNab's Island, and from crossing to main land. It was stated that some of them had been going at large on the island, and washing their clothing in the streams, so that the attention they are now receiving from the police is not at all unnecessary.

"A letter from one of the medical gentlemen on board the *England*, written yesterday morning, says 'all the passengers are removed – some to the Island and some on board the *Pyramus*; which has been turned into a hospital ship.' Thursday night there were six deaths on the Island; on board the *Pyramus*, six bodies were carried up before 9 pm, and on Friday morning, twelve were dead, and fifteen reported dying. The writer says such a state of dirt, disease and misery, as the passengers are in, no one could believe without seeing it. The disease is wholly confined to the steerage passengers, not one of the cabin passengers having been attached with it. We may state that the medical staff from the city who volunteered to go to the assistance of the *England*'s passengers, consists of Dr. Slayter, Health Officer of this port, Dr. Garvie, Dr. Gossip, and Mr. F. Garvie, medical student. They have been instrumental in relieving, to a large extent, the sufferings of the unfortunate passengers, and the public will be glad to learn that they have thus far escaped the contagion. It is reported from the *Pyramus* today that eleven deaths occurred last night."

While searching through my papers, I also read the account of the Archbishop of Halifax's role in the cholera ship affair.

On the morning of April 13, at a wharf along the Halifax waterfront, a Customs officer named Hagarty readied a skiff to be rowed to the S.S. *England*. He waited with the pilot until he saw, walking down the wharf, his travel companion, Archbishop Thomas L. Connolly. Thomas Connolly was a celebrated figure in Nova Scotia. In addition to ministering to the needs of Halifax's Catholics, Connolly had become increasingly political over the years and made a name for himself as an ardent defender of the Irish. By the time of the cholera outbreak, he had become an outspoken champion of the Confederation movement. In fact, some years later, he would be described as the "god-father" of Confederation.

He was, according to those who knew him, a uniquely tenacious and disciplined man of humble origins. Born and raised in County Cork, Ireland, young Connolly fell under the tutelage of Father Theobald Mathieu, known as the "Apostle of Temperance." Mathieu was impressed with the natural talents and noteworthy tenaciousness of Connolly and enthusiastically encouraged his studies. Later, as Connolly distinguished himself as a student, Mathieu arranged to have him sent to Capuchin College in Rome. There, Connolly did well. In 1838, he was ordained as a priest in Lyons, France, from where he travelled back to Ireland to work in a Dublin prison. After four years, he accompanied Bishop William Walsh as a personal secretary to Halifax, Nova Scotia, where he served as Vicar-General of the Halifax Diocese until he was appointed Bishop of Saint John, serving for seven years, after which, in 1859, he was appointed Archbishop of Halifax.

By the time he became archbishop, Connolly was well aware of the hundred-year history of religious and ethnic tensions in the city. In the immediate years leading up to Connolly's appointment, Halifax had seen a series of Protestant versus Catholic flashpoints, including Joseph Howe's efforts in 1854 to recruit Irishmen to fight in the Crimean War; the controversial education bill of 1856 (the Irish were concerned that equitable schooling would not be provided to Catholics); and, most seriously, the fallout from the Gourley Shanty Riot in June of 1856. That riot in particular had created a violent schism between the Catholics and Protestants.

It began on the holiday of Corpus Christi, in the spring of 1856, when a group of Catholic railway workers had taken the day off to attend Mass. When the group returned to work, Protestant workers began taunting the Catholics with derogatory comments about their religion. Tensions rose, then simmered. On the following day, when the skies opened up and rain began falling, work was temporarily suspended. The labourers – Catholic and Protestant – retreated to a small shanty owned by a man named Gourley. There, with tempers still hot, words were again exchanged, then blows, and within a few minutes, a full-blown riot broke out. Though no one died, the fight was bloody enough to leave some with injuries that "the victims bore to their graves."

The matter might well have been forgotten, except that Joseph Howe – never shy about his anti-Irish feelings – exploited the fight to his own ends. With no subtle irony, Howe announced to the press that the Gourley Shanty riot "was an attack upon Protestants, prompted by Catholic intolerance, and bigotry, with the intention to rule the Province and dominate Protestantism." Of course, no proof of such bigotry was ever offered by Howe, but then again, none was needed in a city already primed for anti-Irish hatred. Indeed, Howe had spent many years using his newspaper, *The NovaScotian*, to paint an unflattering portrait of the Irish Catholic community in Halifax and Nova Scotia. In the tense atmosphere of the Fenian threat and the push for Confederation, Howe's attack amounted to fuel on the fire. Amid this growing tension, Archbishop Connolly became political to protect his flock and tribe.

When asked by Howe in 1854 what he thought about Howe's speech favouring "colonial representation in the British Parliament," Connolly responded sharply. "I have carefully read over your speech on the Union of Colonies," he said, "and it would be in bad taste to say to you what I thought of it." No doubt, Connolly's Irish background made him suspicious about any relationship that had Nova Scotia under the direct political control of the British Parliament. Few were surprised, then, when Connolly made his feelings known about the union of Canada.

"I am deeply convinced that instead of being split up and isolated and nameless and miserable as we are," he wrote, "the sooner we are united in all these Provinces the better. If we remain in status quo our very weakness will tempt our Yankee friends to pay us a visit ... We may have to pay more taxes but we shall have more trade and more development of our resources and more self respect, a bigger position in the eyes of the world and a name to go abroad with."

It is clear, though unsaid, that Connolly saw the potential betterment of Nova Scotia's Irish Catholic community in

Confederation. In addition to his fear of the British, Connolly also feared the Americans. He believed that, should the Northern states defeat the Confederacy in the U.S. Civil War, Nova Scotia could be potentially absorbed by the United States. His many trips to New England, and his awareness of its Irish radicals and their plans, only confirmed his fears. He was convinced that it was only a matter of time before the Americans invaded Canada. Such fears made him a staunch supporter of Tupper's proposed Canadian union. Consequently, the glebe house in Halifax became the site of many visits from Confederate sympathizers and agents.

In January of 1865, Connolly publicly supported the idea of Confederation after one local newspaper suggested that the Catholic Church was harbouring Fenians and supporting Fenian activities. On February 13, Connolly defended the loyalty of Irish Catholics in Nova Scotia, suggesting that the Fenian threat was cause for supporting the Union of Canada. "I feel it a duty," he wrote, "to declare myself unequivocally in favour of Confederation as cheaply and as honourably obtained as possible, but Confederation at all hazards and at all reasonable sacrifices."

Clearly, Confederation was not on the archbishop's mind on the morning he and Hagarty rowed to the *England*. Upon arrival at the ship, the archbishop was told by Captain Grace that he could not board. Instead, Captain Grace spoke with the archbishop at what one newspaper described as "hailing distance." The captain gave the archbishop a frank assessment of the situation and of the state of the emigrants. In turn, the archbishop listened, acknowledged the captain's challenges, and promised to send help. Then he and Hagarty returned to Halifax.

At the glebe house later that evening, Connolly gave much thought to the best plan of action. In doing so, he had called on Father Alexander McIsaac, who ministered to the parishioners at Saint Patrick's parish. At forty-one years of age, Father

McIssac – born and raised in Inverness, Cape Breton, and a priest since 1845 – was a pugnacious sort, short and thick with a round face, close-cropped hair, and a flattened nose. He came readily at the archbishop's call.

After entering the glebe house and making his way to the archbishop's study, Father McIsaac inquired after the cholera ship, about which he had been reading in the newspapers. He listened as the archbishop related the details Captain Grace had imparted to him. When the archbishop finished, McIsaac immediately volunteered to minister to the sick and dying. Connolly, no doubt pleased by the offer, accepted. Within the hour, with Father McIsaac not "even delaying to secure clothing," the two men made their way to the waterfront and onto a waiting skiff, which took them out to the *England*.

When they arrived at the island, Father McIsaac and Archbishop Connolly took note of one vessel unloading the empty coffins onto the *England*. At the same time, they saw two other boats whose decks were filled with coffins full. They came alongside the *England*, and Captain Grace again spoke to Connolly and the priest from hailing distance. The captain welcomed Father McIsaac, who turned in the skiff to say goodbye to Connolly. McIsaac then stood, reached for the ladder, and began the climb to the deck.

As he made his way up, a coffin being lowered to another boat let go its lid. Before anyone could stop it, the body slipped out of the box and fell toward Father McIsaac. Instinctively, the priest pulled himself close to the ship, but not close enough. The body struck him on the head as it fell, twisting outward, and then crashing onto the waiting boat below. The horrified archbishop watched the startled Father McIsaac, who held tight to the ladder. But the persistent priest was undaunted. He collected himself, waved again at the archbishop, and then continued up the ladder and onto the deck. Then the archbishop, for the second time that day, headed back to Halifax.

On board the *England*, Father McIsaac followed Captain Grace below deck and spent some time assessing those still there. Then he left the cholera ship and travelled to the *Pyramus* where he ministered to the dying. Finally, he made his way to the island, where he walked among the makeshift tent villages, attending to the sick, dying, and dead. For the next two nights, Father McIsaac slept among the emigrants on beds of straw, until, on the third night, he was moved with the doctors to the Hugonin house.

As I thumbed through the papers in my hand, I came across the longest letter from Dr. Slayter to Dr. Tupper, dated April 13, 1866. In riveting detail, the letter described the events of the previous day, though likely – given the harried handwriting and the confused sentence structure – the sleepless days and nights had melded together. Plainly, John Slayter was exhausted. "Steamship *England*," he began, "April 13th 1866, To the Honourable Provincial Secretary.

"Sir, I must apologize for not answering more fully into our trials in my reports to you, but our time is so much occupied that one has no consciousness [of what one has done for a day or two]. For instance, last night one of each Gossip, Garvie, [and] myself had to attend to the sick in the Hulk as nurses; haul up about 15 dead bodies, put some of them in coffins and clean two decks of ship although the sick are dying fast. The disease is not spreading on shore. Some have been seized amongst those sent from *Pyramus*. Thus from exposure maybe before, but for want of tents accommodation [though] we now have that rum. There was plenty of room for them all in the tents but the building would not allow more than a certain number in these tents."

I tried to imagine the sheer size of the undertaking. More than a thousand people were being moved from ship to shore or ship to ship, while others were being attended to for their illnesses, and others still were being buried on Thrumcap. The different languages spoken among the emigrants no doubt made some communication difficult, and tensions must have run high. Fearing the illness, some emigrants ran to the woods, heading south. Others ran north, causing great distress among the soldiers in Fort Ives. Still others pushed east, with the hope of escaping across the narrow channel to Eastern Passage.

Matters worsened as growing ethnic tensions among the emigrants threatened violence. "The German and Irish [will not] agree," recalled Slayter. "[T]hey, the Irish, won't allow the Germans to come in their district. I am going to have the shanties put up on the Green Hill [in the south]. You have better house accommodations for 150 or more." Still, there were those among the emigrants, said Slayter, who helped to keep the peace. "They have two priests – one Irish; the other French. And they have acted splendidly; their presence and they seem to be everywhere at all times amongst their flock encouraging them, does and has done a great deal in [controlling] the panic. They think no more of shouldering a dead body, than of eating their breakfast. Their cheerful spirits and courage from the commencement of the disease is the admiration of all on board."

I imagined Slayter walking among the tents, listening to the emigrants talk and addressing their many needs. In the midst of the dying and dead, Drs. Slayter, Garvie, and Gossip were ironically called upon to bring life into the world. "We have had three midwifery cases," said Slayter, "to vary our professional duties." For a time, I imagined the deliveries and the mothers in their tents, holding their newborns. What fear they must have felt for their newborns in this place.

The job of burying the dead seemed an unending task. "This morning [on the 12th of April] at 4 o'clock," recounted Slayter, "I got a crew of English miners who consented to go down and dig graves and then send for bodies for burial." Again and again, Slayter was called upon to row the coffins to

Thrumcap and drag them on shore to the graves. The experience must have been exhausting and heartbreaking. Yet, for all of his concerns, Slayter seemed particularly worried for the children.

"More distressing [stories] have occurred here," he wrote to Tupper. "Children [are] left orphans. Five poor little children are alone by themselves. They were clinging to their dead mother not to be left alone. It knocked the strongest person in the crowd as [in] another place you would [see] brothers sisters husbands and wives all sick trying to help one another – little children laying sick with no relation or friend to help them – you may suppose we have something to do, and if our arrangement have not been perfect, we have good excuse for any ill." One wonders if Slayter thought of his own children and of his wife back home on Argyle Street.

Unable to find the right words, Slayter seemed overwhelmed. "It is impossible to magnify what has occurred here," he wrote. "The captain, two officers, including the medical department of the ship are doing their uttermost. And I firmly believe, had they gone to [New York], they would have been now knocking about [the] Atlantic without sufficient help to manage the ship and a perfect charnel house.

"A great many more children have been afflicted. The first few days … no women were attacked but afterward it became general. The report from the island first received is very favourable so far as the disease are concerned but the people are worse than beasts. Whole families, women and children including those poor little orphans were excluded from tents. Knock up shanties as quick as possible or else our community will get an awful name abroad.

"Dr. Gossip and Frank Garvie – I do not believe have had one hour's rest since coming down. (This they kept quiet to prevent their friends from feeling anxious about them. I have two of Cunard's men sick this morning. I will report this evening how they are getting on."

Slayter seemed near breakdown. As his letter concluded, his thoughts became increasingly jumbled. Trying to maintain some sense of hope, he put forward a brave face. But his words betrayed him. "I am reporting of this," he wrote, "I write of a bright account of our gratification to prevent anxiety. This is the style of life I like and as jolly as possible. Allow I cannot begin to wallow in the pathetic post of the business."

Slayter then tried to dissuade himself that this was an epidemic of cholera. "[Performing] post mortem in a few cases when I get time," he speculated, "I feel doubtful whether this is true Asiatic Cholera. [More likely the illness was caused by] infected meat from England, overcrowding, and poor institutions. I think in the course [of] stormy weather, the ship had [gotten] worse. All will end sick. I think plenty of medical assistance here ... from professional work and we must try and pull through without asking for other ... wanted to get men from the admiral; two sisters of charity, but I would only listen to the risk incurred. I am in hopes the work is over."

Perhaps aware of his dark tone, he wrote, "You will think I am cranking but you want some particulars and I hope some disinterested person who has seen the worst of it will give you an account of the affair." But his mood was fragile. He saw the situation getting out of hand and sniped at those who were sent to help. "The police," he wrote, "I begin to think are about – as [useful] while in their position afloat – as the 5th wheel to a coach by all means. If you can get a force round the wood I think it would be prudent." He finished with a surprising barb, an act of transference perhaps for someone who had clearly come up against the limits of one man's ability to control fate. "German emigrants," he wrote tersely, "are filthy."

"I have the honour," he signed off, "of being your servant, Dr. Slayter."

Aware that the day was passing, I placed the papers back in my bag, and from my seat on the tree trunk, I stared north down what seemed a faint muddy path. As I did, I considered Slayter's words and his state of mind. Exhausted, he faced challenges beyond his control. And yet, he would not concede to the chaos, to the darkness that fast enveloped him.

Still, as sometimes is the nature of fate, Slayter would soon face an even greater challenge.

8

Diet

"DIET – Rice water, arrowroot, Sydenham's White Decoction, crust water, chamomile tea, are the best articles for a day or two after the attack is controlled. Chamomile is very valuable in restoring the tone of the stomach."
– Dr. Cyrus Hamlin, Constantinople, 1865

Accepting that I could no longer continue south, I left my tree trunk and travelled north to try my luck along another route. This time, I would head west to the beach at the end of Searchlight Road and then south to Thrumcap. As I marched intently along the faint path, I contemplated the events of 1866.

During the day on April 14, the situation on the island had deteriorated rapidly. Efforts to organize the passengers all but collapsed. The tents in which the emigrants were to stay were not being constructed fast enough to accommodate the numbers, nor were the emigrants being properly quarantined on the south side of the island away from the permanent residents. As the snow and rain continued to fall, matters only worsened. The Germans and Irish grew increasingly suspicious of each other. And both groups were suspicious of anyone – German or Irish – whom they did not know. Food grew scarce. So did potable water.

As Reverend Ambrose Martin remembered, "While I was taking my turn through the German section, I nearly stumbled over a man and his wife, locked in each other's arms, cold, black, and lifeless. A few yards farther on another woman had drawn her shawl over her face, and had laid down and died."

Martin also recalled, "Two cholera tents were spread aside from the healthy; we really needed them, and they were soon filled up, but very rapidly thinned. When stricken the malady was so violent in many cases that the unfortunate creatures had scarcely the power to indicate a passer-by in their present state. On the hospital ship the mortality was very great. It was impossible to rally their courage; when they felt themselves seized by the scourge they seemed powerless, and immediately gave themselves up to despondency."

John Slayter lamented the worsening situation. "The arrangements here are very bad for want of help [from] the people on shore," a discouraged Slayer wrote to Tupper on April 14. "Some of those ashore are dying of starvation. When food is sent off, the strong seize it and the sick and all who have not friends suffer having no food for two days." Slayter worked quickly to shore up the fraying edges of civility. "I had to swear in special constables," he noted, "and have good arrangements made for their getting food."

The sheer weight of the experience was crushing. "Last night was very bad," Slayter wrote. "Frank Garvie and myself were ashore almost all night getting women and children in from [the] woods, they having been refused admittance into the tents on account of them not having friends." The children wandered, frightened and aimless, desperately trying to find comfort where they could.

Slayter, too, worried about the deteriorating relationships. It is worth noting that, in writing to Tupper, Slayter's hand feverishly raced across the page, his script growing increasingly spidery and thin, his thoughts streaming out in near random order. His letter of April 14 was particular in this respect. After filling both sides of a small, off-white piece of paper, he turned the page ninety degrees and continued writing across the words already written. Although this style of writing was not uncommon in an age when paper was, at times, hard to come by and expensive, the cross writing, and the near incoherent nature of the sentences, added to the strange sense that he had been pushed to his limits.

"The effect on the community," he wrote, "you can easily imagine as for remaining at the upper part of the island at present with the help we have is an impossibility and it would be fatal [to transfer] the whole crowd. The boat we took the bodies off to bury. We could no bring back. I have now to bury hand the ship. I have to direct everything and cannot at present say the number of dead."

Still, despite these challenges, he felt some degree of confidence that the disease could be isolated. "If I carry out my arrangements," he told Tupper, "the disease will be certainly at an end. It is now like a hay barn on fire. The flames have charred part of the material being consumed, but requiring a wind to set it going and though wind we had all night, another such would leave the island a mass of dead bodies without help to bury them."

As Slayter wrote, his spidery script became increasingly difficult to read, with many of his words illegible. "I forgot one half," he scrawled with no use of punctuation or capitalization. "I have to write to you [in] about in two days [as] we will have [some period] of time. I am going to follow my own plans out. There is no danger of communicating disease now with my arrangements. I put the women and children in dry places … I think I told you what [unclear] and I can't guide me properly before there is now such [also unclear]. [We] will get through who have been separated and are perfectly healthy and off to New York. I will write to you again about that …"

Later in the day, Slayter wrote another letter in which he seemed more clear-headed, suggesting perhaps that he had managed a few hours of sleep. In this letter, he offered Tupper his plan of action for the children. "I present for your inspection my Commission as Magistrate," he wrote again on April 14, "and beg to state that I require immediate possession of the Houses and Barns occupied by the military as their use is necessary for quarters for women and children on McNab's Island under any care, the community on shore being in danger of infection and the lives of the emigrants at the other. If you have no authority to comply with my order will you let me know if I will receive opposition from your command in taking them. In taking this step I will make immediate arrangements for the accommodation of your Command. I would furthermore request that a guard be placed around the shore from Captain Hugonin's Wharf to the Battery called Ive's Battery to prevent escape of the Emigrants. If you have not sufficient force at your command to form this guard, I will at once send for more then."

In the comfort of his Province House office, Charles Tupper must have soberly acknowledged to himself the real possibility of emigrants escaping to the mainland, and the possibility of the contagion spreading. He requested that the military be used to ensure the execution of the quarantine.

This order must have come quickly as is evidenced in Lieutenant R.H. Dunning's report to Tupper by day's end of the 14th. "I have the honour to state for the information of the Major General Command," Dunning wrote, "that I arrived here yesterday with my detachment and took over the house and quarters according to orders. I found the whole of the emigrants encamped at the North End of the Island (about 7 or 8 hundred yards south of Ive's battery) and at the South End of the island as I suppose. The Guard therefore which I was ordered to furnish in Captain Lyttleton's Barn would be of no use. I have therefore placed a line of flying sentries above the wharf and North End of the island to keep the people as far as lies in my power on the North-West corner, but as the road where the sentries are posted is about half a mile long and very little cleared around either side it will be impossible to keep sufficient guarded during the night ..."

On the island, Dunning approached the situation decisively and moved the emigrants efficiently. It was also clear from his reports that the S.S. *England* still had passengers aboard. "Dr. Slayter reported no deaths yesterday on board the steamship *England*," he reported, "but says the epidemic is very bad on board the *Pyramus* and the condition of those on shore very bad chiefly caused by exposure to the cold and wet. He also adds that unless proper and efficient shelter can be obtained immediately, he does not see how the disease can abate." As Dunning's troops made some accounting of the emigrants, it also became clear that many had attempted an escape. "I also ascertained this morning that some emigrants (now not known)," he reported, "escaped in a boat from the north end of the island after nine o'clock last night but it is impossible to say in what direction they have gone."

Prepared to do what was necessary to restore order among the more than one thousand emigrants, Dunning appeared to have been well-received. "I do not see any cause to apprehend resistance or violence from any of the men encamped on the island," he reported, "who have at present been most ready to obey the orders of my sentries who have been as civil as possible in consistence with their duty, but on no account to let any strange person within fifty yards of him."

On that same day, Saturday, April 14, while Lieutenant Dunning was establishing order on the north end of the island, and while Drs. Slayter, Garvie, and Gossip were attending to the sick and burying the dead, Father McIsaac spent much of his day among the ill, giving comfort where possible and, among those who were dying on the *Pyramus*, listening to confessions.

In McNab's Cove, Archbishop Connolly had rowed out for another firsthand report. He was disheartened by what he saw and heard. With his own eyes he watched the steady succession of coffins lowered from the *Pyramus* and the *England* into smaller rowboats for the long trip around the Mauger's Beach lighthouse to Thrumcap. So, too, he noted labourers working on the bluff above the cove, called Hugonin Point, digging a large trench for an expeditious burial site.

From the deck of the *England*, Captain Grace told the archbishop of the grim, worsening situation. The scarcity of food was of great concern. He described one incident of the morning after the arrival of Drs. Gossip and Garvie, when both had assisted in serving food to the emigrants from a large pot of soup. The emigrants' hunger was such that the "maddened crowd" caused a brief riot and "upset the pot, which emptied its contents onto the ground." Some were so desperately hungry that they clawed at the dirt for nourishment. Captain Grace also told Connolly of the orphaned children who were shunned by the other emigrants for fear that they carried cholera. The news distressed Connolly. As he rowed back to Halifax late that day, he again pondered the best means to help.

The next morning, on April 15, after services at St. Mary's cathedral, the archbishop called together a meeting of the parish priests and the Sisters of Charity in his glebe house parlour, where he described what he had heard and seen. In particular, he spoke with great emotion about the desperate people who "were in a state of fear and excitement" and about the "many poor children, whose parents had been carried off by the pestilence, [and] had no one to care for them." Solemnly, he asked if any gathered would go to the island. Specifically, he looked to the Sisters of Charity and asked if they "would volunteer to go and take care of those children."

In what must have been an emotional moment, every Sister present "begged to be sent." The archbishop, no doubt moved, chose two of the Sisters, Sister Mary Clare Connelly, a young but experienced member of the order, and novice Sister Mary Vincent Power, "a cheerful generous soul, before whom difficulties disappeared [and who] embraced this work with the same earnest generosity, while her sunny spirit made her see and enjoy the ridiculous no matter when it appeared."

The archbishop then told the Sisters to "make some preparation in the way of sewing materials, buttons, etc., and all the little necessaries they could carry for they were going to some little cabin in which His Grace was not quite sure there was a chimney." He said they should be "very warmly clad and ready to start at 8:30 next morning."

Sister Mary Clare later remembered that the crisis in the city had collided with the tensions felt between the Irish and English. "The greatest fear and excitement prevailed in the city," she later recalled, "and all the daily papers that evening commented in of terms admiration on the spirit that led the priests and Sisters so ready to risk their lives in the cause of charity. No Protestant minister volunteered to go there and the one who was a passenger aboard the fatal ship shut himself in his room and was not seen after the cholera broke out."

By Sunday the matter of containing the emigrants remained pressing. "I beg to inform you that yesterday evening one of my sentries reported a boat at the north end of the island which he thought was for the purpose of either communicating with emigrants or taking them off the island," Lieutenant Dunning reported to Slayter. "I went there with some of my detachment and found a boat on the shore and two men named Coon who reside on the North End part of the island, standing close by who informed me they were going to Halifax for provisions for the Emigrants. I hauled the boat up and [forbade] them to leave the island. I have also good reason for supposing a man named Ulender supplies spirits at his house. I also beg to suggest that a boat anchored in McNab's Cove on the North End of the island would be a great safe guard in watching the boats leaving the island as my sentries are insufficient to perform this duty."

As for Slayter, though exhausted physically and emotionally, he felt, perhaps for the first time since arriving at the island, some faint cause for optimism. "I have not yet got reports of the mortality last night," he wrote, "but think the disease is rapidly on the decrease. I have sworn in the special constables amongst the passengers and the provisions [which had recently arrived] are served to all hands." The special constables controlled the crowds on the island but also ensured that no one left.

"I have heard reports, with what foundation I can't say," Slayter also wrote, "that some have escaped ashore. I know they are supplied with liquor. I will try and find out the parties and make heavy penalties for the offender and punish the same. Send handbills to Lawlor's Island and Eastern Passage. The guard is not strong enough for guard duty. No rouse will occur but they are required to prevent communication. Some might be stationed at the North Battery. The police are not worth their salt and the responsibility of communication with the shore must rest with them. I will address particulars to Mayor. The less you will require me to write for two days the better as my time can be more properly spent."

Among the emigrants, Slayter felt he had finally gained some ground in organizing the tent community. He decided to accommodate the ethnic split that had occurred. "Today, I will have boards laid down in every tent – in tents separated at considerable distance from one another and trenches all around to drain. Mr. Morrow is going to send today four large pots. Two for German Town, and two for Irish Town, for you must know we are beginning to assume the shape of a tent village. Today, I am going to address the population on the necessity of boards of health to keep the place in the best sanitary condition."

Still, of the operation to feed the emigrants and to bury the dead, Slayter felt continually overwhelmed. "We have only about forty working, that is for cooking grub, manning boats, burying dead, and a hundred and one things. You have no idea. They are up from four o'clock to late at night. The Captain and officers are working little men at night. The Captain is walking in his room half the night in the greatest excitement, grieved about the condition of his passengers. During working hours, he is a true British Sailor, strict orders were given about everything being burned."

Slayter's bigotry, already revealed in comments about the German emigrants, was shown again in his exhaustion. Perhaps, too, he had been affected by the omnipresent threat of a Fenian invasion. "When I am attending to the sick," he wrote, "I can't be accountable for the acts of some emigrants. The Irish are rank Fenians and their ranks are being depleted."

I considered Slayter's bigotry as I walked along Rifle Range Trail, the mud of the path clinging thickly to my shoes. No doubt Slayter's encampment was similarly thick with mud, the emigrants constantly wiping it from their feet and clothes. For a time, I think of Henry Wenner and his sisters, Patrick and Mary Healy and their children, Pieter De Jong, Jr. and his brothers and wives and children, of Aris Eelman and Klaas Vlaming, of Oliver Bacon Harding and his brothers, and of Reverend Ambrose Martin. In their accounts, they offered few descriptions of the camps. Only Reverend Martin and Father McIsaac gave some indication of the chaotic mess of "German Town" and "Irish Town." Still, I thought, despite the horror of the situation, human nature surely must have had them settling into a strange rhythm of sleeping and eating and quiet worrying. All the emigrants by now had been touched by the illness.

And most likely, all had spent their hours and days watching over the welfare of their friends and family.

By the morning of April 16, Slayter was feeling great pressure from Charles Tupper and Lieutenant Governor Williams for more information. By his own admission, he struggled to find the time to recount the day's events.

"The governor wants a report twice a day but work is a necessity, news in town a luxury," he wrote, perhaps gently rebuking Tupper's request for more information. "I will do my best but the hours must be changed to eleven o'clock and six o'clock. You had better appoint Dr. Barrow and any town doctors to dream up a list of questions concerning everything you want to know. Have each be on a sheet of letter paper by itself … and I will answer them one by one from which you can get up a report quicker than we can do it. The fewer on the committee the better, as doctors differ and waste time. In two days, we will be in perfect order." As an aside, Slayter added, "I would advise you to put a schooner quarantine in the harbour in front of Georges Island and anything found such as dead bodies or clothing to go ashore and bury the same."

At the same time, Slayer wrestled with the pressing concerns of the ever-increasing number of bodies. "There is a young person by the name of Robert," he wrote to Tupper, "who is in for anything and will undertake any job of [burying] the bodies [that] are reported along the shore. Let them sail down and attend to the same. There is no danger from contagion after death."

Regarding the newspaper reports that bodies were being tossed over the side of the ship, Slayter wrote, "The only time we threw bodies over was when we were crowded and busy landing passengers and the cause of their floating was the poorly put together coffins sent by Cunard and Co. Those buried without coffins and the coffins from the poorhouse, I will stake my reputation will not appear until the last trumpet sounds. They were heavily weighted and their bodies no worse food for fish than deaths from any other cause and how many bodies are immersed to rise no more at all times."

As if all the cholera deaths were not enough to worry about, Slayter was now confronted with another tragedy. "One of Cunard's men, Pat Reardon, fell overboard the other night from the side of the hulk," he reported. "He fished himself up with a boat hook, but he got his lungs full of water. Inflammation set in and he died last night. He got the rites of the church from Father McIsaac. When convenient we doctors want [to allay] the causes of grumbling ashore. I will arrange a plan when I get time."

For the remainder of that day, Slayter attended to the dying on board the *Pyramus*. When he took some time to rest and eat that evening, he once more took up his pen and wrote to Charles Tupper.

"There are six doctors here, five believe the disease cholera, but I do not and will give you my reasons," wrote Slayter emphatically. "1st – none of us know anything from experience about the disease. 2nd – There is very little pain and purging. Some die passing thin feculent stool. They have cramps in stomach and legs, but not to any extent.

"Symptoms: lung sick, cold on surface, vomiting and purging, stupor; but as first stage, when roused, brighten up. Hands and feet go purple, pulse small from the beginning, tongue whitish but not thick, but furred, some suppression of urine. Some die from collapse. When dead, legs and hands twisted and very hard to straighten out in coffins. The ship's doctors say the collapse is so quick that time is not allowed for cramps, much purging, etc.

"I say [the] 1,300 have been battered down in stormy weather and from air filth a disease has been engendered which is at once eradicated by proper sanitary regulations. I have to go at once to the island and must stop my report." Having finished the letter and sent it via skiff to the city, Slayter returned to his work among emigrants of the tent camps.

As I continued walking, I imagined Slayter watching the orphaned children wander about. I wondered again if he thought of his own children in the city. How far away they must have seemed, not only in space but also in time and context. Just days before – was it just days? – he had been celebrating a birthday with family and friends, toasting a successful career, and looking forward to the birth of his fifth child. And now he walked among the dead and dying, listening to the myriad moans and cries of the fearful. Again and again, he looked into eyes that spoke of desperation and resignation. He must have been sorely tempted to write a letter to his wife, to tell her how much he loved her, to tell her of the progress he felt he was making, and to assure her that all would be well. If indeed he wrote this letter, no record of it remains.

As I considered what Slayter's letter might have said, I came upon Searchlight Road, and without breaking stride or looking back at the path from which I had come, I turned left and plunged straight ahead toward the water.

9

The Typhoid Fever

"THE TYPHOID FEVER – A typhoid state for a few days will follow all severe cases. There is nothing alarming in this. It has very rarely proved fatal. Patience and careful nursing will bring it all right. The greatest danger is from drinking too freely. When the patient seemed to be sinking, a little brandy and water, or arrowroot and brandy have revived him. In this terrible visitation of the cholera we have considered ourselves perfectly armed and equipped, with a hand-bag containing mixture No. 1, mixture No. 2, (for vomiting, etc.) a few pounds of powdered mustard, a bottle of brandy, and a paper of chamomile flowers, and a paper of gum arabie. I lay no claim to originality in recommending this course of treatment, and have adopted it from suggestions of able and experienced physicians. Having been the only Doctor of many poor families living near me, I have tried various remedies recommended by physicians, but I have found none to be at all compared with the above. During the recent cholera I cannot find that any treatment has been so successful as this."

– Dr. Cyrus Hamlin, Constantinople, 1865

Searchlight Road descended steeply down a rocky slope that offered an expansive view of the ocean. As I walked, I watched the water as it entered the harbour, rolling and cresting in a broad clutch of whitecaps. At that distance, and with some imagination, the whitecaps looked like a mass of surfacing sea monsters malevolently swimming toward the city.

The image reminded me that in August of 1853, Peter McNab IV walking near the beach at the north end of the island, was reported by the *NovaScotian* to have seen a sea serpent. "At 6 1/2 o'clock this morning, when returning from McNab's Island," Peter McNab recounted, "I saw a Sea Serpent over 20 feet long, between the Red Buoy and the North West point of the Island moving very rapidly. It greatly resembled a large eel – had a very small head, raised 2 or 3 inches above the water, and it moved in an undulating motion." For half an hour, McNab claimed, this "sea serpent" swam in wide circles, even coming within a hundred yards of the shore.

It occurred to me as I watched the whitecaps crest and disappear that people often ascribed to what was unfamiliar the title of "monster." And I wondered, frankly, if the relative isolation of the island had gotten the better of Peter McNab IV. After all, in 1873, McNab was arrested and tried for the crime of "feloniously cutting and wounding and doing grievous bodily harm." Just whom it was that he tried to "cut, wound, and do grievous bodily harm" to remains unclear. Still, history records that McNab was promptly convicted of his crime. Later, after tipping fully into insanity while in prison, he was sent to Mount Hope Asylum where, not long afterward, he passed away.

While thinking of this violent tale of island madness, I came upon a squared, cement building, tucked amid the trees and tall grass a few yards off Searchlight Road. As with the other buildings on the island, this one was clearly of World War Two vintage. The cement had cracked and chipped, and the metal rods once enveloped by the cement were now exposed and rusted a deep orange. Despite not having seen any sign of civilization since the strange cement and iron wall at the end of Rifle Range Trail, this block-shaped curiosity would not have caused me much concern except that, upon closer examination, I noticed – running from the cement blockhouse to a nearby tree – a clothesline on which there hung, flapping in the wind, a single t-shirt emblazoned with the iconic face of Che Guevara, complete with beret and beard. Not having seen a soul since leaving Captain Red Beard at Wreck Cove hours earlier, I was admittedly startled at the prospect of meeting another person – particularly at this end of the island.

With some effort at stealth, I edged closer to this odd-looking encampment, noticing that behind a tree, and partly obscured by bushes, was a makeshift tent: a blue plastic tarp pulled over another clothesline, tethered to two trees. On the ground next to the tent was a narrow fire pit with charred logs sticking out of the soft earth. And next to the fire pit, scattered liberally near two tattered lawn chairs, were beer bottles, lots of them – all empty.

Now maybe it was the isolation of the island, or maybe it was the memory of Peter McNab's murderous rampage, or just maybe it was the uncomfortable combination of a tarp tent, revolutionary garb, and recently consumed alcohol, but I found myself wondering about the wisdom of continuing down this narrow path toward a broad swath of jagged rocks and open ocean, from which, oh, I don't know, say, a solitary hiker might never be heard from again. And given that these island revolutionaries – likely inebriated and one possibly shirtless for reasons I did not really want to consider – were nowhere to be found, I decided, quite coincidentally, that this path was unlikely to provide me a successful route to Thrumcap. I reasoned that I should turn around and head back to Rifle Range Trail.

And so I did.

That was when I heard people walking toward me.

Just above a small rise in the path from where I had come, two men appeared, carrying between them a large blue and white cooler. The fellow to the left was tall and beefy with a rounded stomach that bulged out against his otherwise loose t-shirt. And the other, also wearing a loose t-shirt, was shorter and thin, with greying hair pulled back into a ponytail. As they came within a half-dozen yards of me, I was sure I heard the distinct sound of clinking bottles. When we met on the path, the bigger guy offered me a broad, friendly grin, and a hearty "Hello."

I nodded and returned the grin, responding with a short, "Hey." Certainly, I had no reason to think either was anything less than a decent fellow, but admittedly I couldn't stop myself thinking about Ned Beatty in *Deliverance*. After I passed, I did feel just a little guilty for assuming that my fellow hikers were possible backwoods cousins of Georgia bootleggers looking for some down-home fun. But then again, my guilt was not so overwhelming that I turned back to share a beer. So I kept marching back up Searchlight Road toward Rifle Range Trail.

When I reached it, and my heart rate returned to a reasonably calm level, I gave one last look south toward Green Hill and Thrumcap. I knew that nothing remained of the graves dug by Dr. Slayter and others on Thrumcap. The relentless waves had long since eroded the north shore of the island and claimed the hastily buried coffins of the cholera victims. And though I had wanted some firsthand sense of the desolation Dr. Slayter and the others felt, I was satisfied, given my present surroundings and circumstances, that I had captured something of the geographic experience.

Besides, there was still another place where I knew the cholera victims had been buried and where their bones still likely lay – on Hugonin Point, overlooking McNab's Cove. So I turned away from the south end of the island and started hiking north. With the day wearing on, I walked at a determined pace, returning my thoughts to the events of 1866 in general and to Dr. Charles Tupper in particular.

Despite being preoccupied with the crisis on McNab's Island, Charles Tupper was, at the same time, wrestling with the challenge of selling Confederation. For two years, he had worked relentlessly to create the conditions necessary for Nova Scotia to join in a union of other provinces. Throughout that time, he faced an uphill fight.

In 1864, not long after being elected Premier of Nova Scotia, he introduced a resolution in the Nova Scotia assembly, proposing a union of Maritime Provinces. The same resolution had already been proposed and accepted in Prince Edward Island and New Brunswick. Tupper's resolution, however, was voted down.

Without clear approval from the Assembly or Nova Scotians at large, Tupper decided to regroup. He travelled to Charlottetown, Prince Edward Island, in September of 1864. There, with the assembled representatives from across British North America, he again discussed Maritime Union. Yet this conversation was quickly superseded by discussions of a larger union to include Upper and Lower Canada. This discussion was encouraging enough to warrant another conference in Quebec City in October of 1864, at which the details of Canadian union were finally worked out.

And so, on April 10, 1865, one year before the cholera began to rage on McNab's Island and the fear of Fenian attack had reached a mania, Dr. Charles Tupper addressed the Nova Scotia Assembly in a speech that concluded with the following resolution: "Whereas in the opinion of this House it is desirable that a Confederation of the British North American Provinces should take place, resolved therefore that His Excellency the Lieutenant Governor be authorised to appoint delegates to arrange with the Imperial Government a scheme of union which will effectually secure just provision for the rights and interests of this Province and for the Provinces co-operating to have an equal voice in such delegation, Upper and Lower Canada for this purpose being viewed as separate Provinces."

It did not take Confederation opponent Joseph Howe long to respond. "Every Nova Scotian has the right, nay the duty," wrote Howe, "to stand up and defend the institutions of his country against them all." Tupper, perhaps surprised by the degree of antipathy he had again engendered from his fellow Nova Scotians, wisely held back a vote on the resolution for one full year.

This popular antipathy to Confederation came, in part, because the years between 1854 and 1866 were prosperous ones for Nova Scotia. The Reciprocity Treaty of 1854 provided a liberal trade agreement between Nova Scotia and the United States, setting the stage for rapid economic growth. An economy that valued "wood, wind and sail" was a boon for a province whose shipbuilding, fisheries, and timber industries were so productive. Consequently, for Nova Scotians, the idea of Confederation was rightly seen by most with some suspicion. They wondered what this union would take from Nova Scotia rather than give. In particular, the powerful merchant class of Nova Scotia was deeply opposed to union on the grounds that it would likely increase taxation and bring additional tariffs.

Charles Tupper, however, believed that the future was shifting away from the strong economic conditions that made the independent province so strong. And indeed, as 1866 arrived, the Americans, beginning the long road of recovery from the Civil War, did not renew the Reciprocity Treaty. Tupper saw this as a portent. He believed more than ever that Confederation would provide more stable markets in the west.

My musing about Charles Tupper and Confederation was interrupted by a flock of birds overhead and by my arrival at the short path along Culliton Farm Trail to Garrison Road. There I took a break and found a comfortable-looking tuft of grass at the side of the trail. After checking the grass for dryness, I sat, opened my bag, and removed my red folder and the sheets that offered the news of the day.

On April 15, 1866, the *Citizen* reported, "Mrs. Jane Donovan, [had died] in the 92nd year of her age," while Mr. Edward Daly, "a native of the Co. Wexford, Ireland, and for many years a resident of Halifax," passed away "in the 78th year of his age, after a lingering illness. Also in the city, "an inquest was held" regarding "the dead body of a female child found in a garden in Gottingen Street last Saturday morning."

Also there was an "inquest on the body of Mr. W.H. Scott," the bookkeeper who died at home of a gunshot wound to the head. The verdict was not an accidental death as first thought but "suicide during temporary insanity." The paper also noted, "Mr. Keith of the firm of Gordon & Keith had the little finger of his right hand taken off by a moulding machine which he was superintending in their furniture factory this afternoon."

I shuffled through my papers and found additional letters between John Slayter and Charles Tupper. Writing to Tupper, on April 16, Slayter reported again on the number of deaths. "I beg to report of deaths last night on the Hulk and two on the island," he began. "We have only about twelve more to die on the hulk and at most four on the island. The disease I am sure will then be at an end. I have sent for three Sisters of Charity. I will isolate them in a house, vacated men's encampment. The Priests are working very hard allaying the fears of their flock. The sisters are for the protection of the orphans about.

"The cabin passengers want to know if they can take the train at Bedford and proceed on their voyage. There has been no sickness among them and they have been separated from the steerage passengers since the 9th or 10th. They would hire a tug to carry them to Bedford and not come to the city. I consider there is not the slightest danger but as there is considerable excitement ashore about cholera I submit to your judgment without recommending one thing or another.

"I told the Archbishop if you would allow for Pat Reardon's body to come ashore in a leaden coffin and then put in a wooden coffin on the beach, he might have a funeral and gratify his friends. The grave can be dug very deep and these facts put in the newspapers so as to prevent any alarm. Moreover, settle the point yourself.

"Lieutenant Dunning suggests that boats at different points of the island – north, south, east, and west – with boatmen patrolling the water would be the best plan of preventing communication. The Policemen are of no use. I believe they remain on board their schooner night and day."

In Halifax, on the morning of April 16, Sister Mary Clare and Sister Mary Vincent followed the archbishop's instructions and gathered their things. As they finished, Archbishop Connolly knocked at their door. He greeted the sisters warmly and offered to accompany them to the wharf. Then, along with the Mother Superior and the other members of the order, they all walked the three blocks or so to the waterfront. From there the procession marched to Market Wharf with many Halifax citizens watching.

As Sister Mary Clare remembered it, the archbishop "would have this expedition as public as possible for he knows that this courageous charity would give proof of the Catholic faith and elevate religion before the Protestant mind, that at that time so dreaded the fearful scourge, the Asiatic Cholera." The symbolic pushback against the prevailing fear of Fenians could not have been missed. Here, Connolly presented the city's Irish Catholics as saviours.

"On the arrival of the party on the Market Wharf," remembered Sister Mary Clare, "[we] found a crowd of gentlemen, Protestant and Catholic, awaiting [us]. [We] said good-bye to Mother and the Sister who accompanied her, then stepped into the rowboat with all [our] bags and bundles and the Archbishop. The men plied their oars and soon [we] were off leaving the crowd looking after [us], some in admiration, others in surprise at the ease with which [we] rushed to death."

Shifting my position on the grass, I imagined the sight at the Market Wharf, the crowd of anxious well-wishers, the chatter among those waving goodbye. And I imagined the near silence of those in the boat as they moved slowly across the choppy water, making their way toward the island and the S.S. *England*. "The wind was high," Sister Mary Clare later wrote, "and the sea very rough, but once outside the harbour [we] soon came in sight of the fatal ship."

The archbishop ordered the men rowing to come alongside the *England*. There, Captain Grace again greeted all from the deck. The captain told the archbishop that the "the last of the sick" had been "removed to the island and now the work of fumigation was going on board." Thanking the captain, the archbishop and the Sisters made their way to Findlay's Wharf. There, Sister Mary Clare watched "a line of men [who were] carrying coffins on their shoulders." The men were prisoners who had recently been forced to the island to assist in burying the bodies. Later, the Sisters would learn that the bodies were accruing so quickly that the dead "remained for days on the field, the number constantly increasing." Those desperately trying to help the living simply spread "a canvas sail ... over the pile" of bodies "until the labours of the doctors abated a little." Later, when time allowed, the doctors and volunteers would then cover "themselves with disinfectants" and bury "the dead in one common grave or pit" either on Thrumcap or the new trench on Hugonin Point.

At Findlay's Wharf, the Sisters and the archbishop climbed the ladder to the dock where Dr. Slayter greeted them "very cordially." Slayter, though tired and grim, was pleased to see the Sisters. He turned to the archbishop and promised that they would be well cared for. Then he begged their pardon as he had work to do.

The archbishop and the Sisters were taken up the nearby hill to a small cottage. There they "met the caretaker with a horse and cart at the door of his small house, from which he was hurrying away with a few valuables." Graciously, the caretaker had offered the lodge to the Sisters, along with the horse and cart, "for which," Sister Mary Clare noted, "they were thankful, as it was the only house on the island."

Entering the lodge, the Sisters discovered a kitchen "that was a little [more than a] cooking stove, a table, two chairs, a dresser, with a few dishes, and an old sofa." As well, there was "a small bedroom containing a large bedstead with a straw mattress on it and a small table and chair. Upstairs was one attic room which contained three bedsteads, on each one a straw mattress which was a luxury." The house was in a serious state of disrepair. "[We] used [our] cloaks and clothing as coverlets," remembered Sister Mary Clare about the porous state of the residence. "Through the roof, the stars might be seen at night and on the floor the boards were only laid not nailed which meant cautious stepping."

At noon the archbishop ate lunch with the Sisters and then offered them a blessing, "telling them his boat and man would be there each morning to get the news each day from them." The archbishop then departed, leaving the Sisters to organize the modest residence. They arranged their belongings and then "set to work to sweep up the place." As Sister Mary Clare remembered, "The floors were filled with straw that had been pulled out of the mattresses for packing purposes and the broom fortunately was left behind the door." Soon after, Doctor Garvie arrived at the residence and encouraged them to begin work immediately. Garvie had brought with him "two fine Irish girls who were glad to help." The girls "went to work with a will, made a fire, swept the place and would have moved the stove, fire and all, had not the Sisters been on the spot."

Almost immediately the Sisters' residence was visited by a steady stream of doctors and ship officials. "One of them brought four Irish children," recalled Sister Mary Clare, "who had lost their mother. They cried with all their might, the four together." Despite the tears, the Sisters bathed the children. Afterward they looked for clean clothes but found none. "Sister Vincent," continued Sister Mary Clare, "tried to wash some for them, but the Doctor saw the performance when he came in and ordered the clothing to be buried; theirs was too filthy, and besides, the washing was too dangerous."

And so the Sisters sent word to Halifax for children's clothes. By the next morning, Sister Alphonsus arrived on the island with "plenty of clothing for the children." Later other children were brought to the nuns. "Two died," recalled Sister Mary Clare, "one of cholera." That girl was "of twelve years, [and the] eldest sister of four." She was carried from the residence by the doctor "while she writhed in pain."

That same day, April 16, Charles Tupper wrote again to Dr. Slayter. "In reply to your report of today I have to express the great satisfaction afforded by your opinion as to the early extinction for the disease and trust that you will be able to discharge the *England* with as many as possible of the passengers. In the meantime, it is not considered judicious to allow any of the passengers to leave in any other way. Unless there is some special objection … I have applied to the major to carry out your wishes respecting the guard around the shores of the island. If there is any thing required to contribute to the comfort of those around you, do not hesitate to let me know. Collect all the data you can for a full and detailed report upon the whole matter. I think it would create serious alarm if poor Reardon's body were brought at present. If he was buried in a leaden coffin, the body might be subsequently removed, but at present it might do mischief."

In the city, residents were increasingly concerned that cholera would escape to shore. Already rumours of emigrants finding their way to Eastern Passage were rampant, spurred on by the newspapers. On Tuesday, April 17, 1866, the *Citizen* headline read, "THE CHOLERA. Cheering News from the Plague Ship Outbreak of the Cholera in Ferguson's Cove." Ferguson's Cove is located across the harbour from McNab's Cove on the Halifax side.

"On Sunday last," indicated the article, "the cheering intelligence was brought to the city that no more cases of cholera had occurred on board the S.S. *England*, and that no deaths took place the previous night. On Sunday night, however, eight deaths occurred. Yesterday it was understood from official quarters that there were twelve of the patients whom it would be impossible to save, but that the disease was effectually checked, and in a fair way of disappearing from the vessel.

"On Sunday night eight of the passengers, filled with panic and impatient of the quarantine restraint, contrived to seize a boat and got off to the East Halifax Shore. As these fugitives may in their rash retreat carry the trail of the pestilence with them, a strong force of constables has been despatched to pursue and arrest them. One of the gang of hired labourers who went down from the city to clear the ship, unfortunately got intoxicated, and falling overboard was drowned.

"Considerable apprehension has been caused by the report of the discovery of bundles of clothing from the infected ship washed ashore in the harbour. Steps have been taken by the authorities and those in charge of the vessel to prevent such carelessness on the part of the passengers and crew.

"We deeply regret to any that on Sunday symptoms of the contagion appeared in Ferguson's Cove, and all doubts as to the character of the disease were removed by the death of the person attached the same day, under strong choleric symptoms. The authorities have had their attention drawn to the case, and have, we believe, adopted prompt sanitary regulations and precautions in the hope of stopping the progress of the plague in the district.

"The S.S. *England* having been cleared of all her living freight, is now to be thoroughly fumigated. Disinfectants were ordered, especially chloride lime; but we are told that only one barrel of that indispensable disinfectant could be got in Halifax! There must be a strange, a culpable, want of foresight somewhere when this is the case, in the very presence of a near and threatening pestilence."

The *Citizen* also reported that "when the SS *England* arrived at the port the other day, crowded with 1,200 passengers, it was reported that three malignant diseases – Asiatic Cholera, Ship Fever, and Small Pox, were raging on board, that large numbers had died, and scores were dying daily; that the medical officer was down and disabled worn out with fatigue and disease and that the Engineers were also disabled. The ship being ordered out of port did proceed on her voyage by the government.

"Dr. Garvie of the city volunteered his services at once to proceed in the vessel to New York. Afterwards, when it was discovered that the *England* could not proceed, she was permitted to remain at Meagher's Beach where Dr. Garvie, his brother, and Drs. Gossip and Slayter joined her, where they still remain battling with the disease, which is now rapidly disappearing. It will be remembered that this Dr. Garvie is the young man who, on a former occasion having volunteered his services, proceeded to Bermuda in the Cunard steamer, while the Yellow Fever was raging in that Island in all its fury. Such bravery as this speaks for itself and ought to be widely known."

Sitting on my tuft of grass at the side of the path, I found myself wondering: how many residents of Halifax had stayed inside their homes during the outbreak? How many steered clear of the taverns and coffee houses? How many avoided the normally crowded markets or sailor-filled waterfront? Pondering these questions, I was conscious that my back was stiff, so I stood and stretched. Then I turned and looked through my bag for more sheets. For a while longer, I sat again to think about Dr. Slayter as he attended to the sick.

In the early hours of April 17, 1866, Dr. Garvie reached for a small sheet of yellow paper, took up a pen, and composed his first letter to Charles Tupper. "Dear Sir," he began, "I regret to inform you that Dr. Slayter is so seriously unwell that we have but slight hopes of his recovery. He was taken ill Saturday morning and continued to grow rapidly worse. Fearing a serious result before he took to bed, he bade me send you the enclosed letter which will I hope prove satisfactory to you."

Slayter had been called away near midnight. Garvie continued his report. "I am glad to assume that the disease on the Hulk *Pyramus* is rapidly declining. As also on the island. And such is the improvement that with the cooperation of the medical officers of the ship and a passenger physician, there is quite enough medicine and help. We are busily employed in making the people on shore as comfortable as possible and having the Hulk *Pyramus* clean, and burying the dead.

"Should, as I anticipate, Dr. Slayter's case prove fatal, I will at once inform you and await your instructions. I leave it to your own good judgment as to whether the news should be broken to his family at once, but we will all deeply deplore his sickness as he was everywhere. When he could, he gave aid to the sick and did all in his endeavours to do good for all."

Garvie, perhaps unnerved at Slayter's sudden illness, finished his letter with thoughts of his family and the families of his colleagues. "Dr. Gossip, Frank, and myself are quite well," he wrote, "of which please appraise our families as they might be anxious. When you receive this please communicate with me at once. In great haste, your humble servant, J.B. Garvie."

I shuffled the papers in my hand until I located a description of Dr. John Slayter's last hours, recorded by an Irish immigrant, called McCormick, also known as the "Doctor's Mate."

"A German immigrant had just died," this McCormick remembered, "and we were putting him in a coffin, at the foot of which his two dead children had been placed." Slayter had been called away from his letter near midnight. As McCormick recalled, Slayter "had not been well during the day, was then almost completely exhausted." By the time Slayter entered the tent with McCormick and an "Irish Catholic friar who came out as a saloon passenger on the *England* and intended to go to New York," he saw the German emigrant and his two sons already dead.

Slayter and the friar then retrieved a plain, wooden coffin. They set it down just inside the tent and all three worked to place the bodies inside. "The doctor," remembered McCormick, "took the head of the dead German, and I took the feet, and we lifted him into his coffin." But the father's body was too large for the coffin, so Dr. Slayter stepped around the box and tried to rearrange the legs. That was when he felt a sharp pain in his abdomen.

"We were startled to see him fall back and cry out in pain," recalled McCormick, "and he was almost immediately seized with violent vomiting." McCormick and the friar quickly made their way to Findlay's Wharf and "hoisted the signal for a boat from the [*Pyramus*]." Then, returning to the tent, the two helped Slayter to the beach and into a rowboat, which carried all three to the hospital ship. As "a warm friendship had sprung up" among the group, recalled McCormick, "the short row to the ship was the saddest I ever had." McCormick had recently witnessed the death of his friend Pat Reardon "only a couple of days before," and he was grieved at the prospect of witnessing the passing of another friend.

Slayter, "though quite weak," was optimistic on board the *Pyramus*. McCormick said, "It seemed hard to believe that another big, strong, healthy man as he was would not recover." McCormick remained at Slayter's bedside. After thirty minutes, Slayter "was seized with such violent cramps that it was almost impossible to keep in his bunk." McCormick said that he "never saw such awful agony before." Slayter cried out in his pain. He gripped at his stomach and pleaded for water. Then he began to suffer from intense "cramps in the legs."

McCormick continued to watch Slayter deteriorate. "It was enough to make one's ears bleed," he said, "to see him suffer and to feel then that so little could be done to relieve him." After a time, "he became completely worn out." Then, as with so many victims before him, Slayter's body grew cold, turning "a purplish hue," and his eyes soon began to sink "back into his head."

Slayter must have known he was dying. In a "voice so husky that he could hardly speak," he said goodbye to his friends. Then, in a harsh "whisper," he "mentioned something about his wife and children," but the voice had grown so weak that his message was unclear. His final minutes were spent in "a sort of trance." Then, when his body could no longer maintain itself under such stress "his brave heart ceased to beat." As McCormick recalled it, "[T]he time between the beginning of his attack until it was ended by death could not have been more than six hours."

Word of Slayter's death travelled quickly to the city. The newspapers read, "Dr. Garvie reported this forenoon to the Government that Dr. Slayter died on board the plague ship at a quarter to ten o'clock this morning. He took ill yesterday morning, and sank rapidly. This new feature in the pestilential calamity has touched all hearts with profound sorrow for the loss of a brave physician, who went calmly and courageously to his post of duty, and died in his efforts to stay the plague from spreading to the city. While we deeply sympathize with his bereaved family, we cannot forget that the heroic grandeur of such a death will make the memory of Dr. Slayter an heirloom to his countrym en. Dr. Garvie testifies feelingly to the energy and humanity displayed by his departed comrade in succoring the sick and the dying on the fatal ship.

"It is stated that Dr. Garvie himself has had an attack and has recovered; and that Dr. Gossip and Mr. Frank Garvie, medical student, are quite well though very hard worked. We believe, indeed, that these young men ought to be relieved or reinforced, in their exhausting superintendence of an infected multitude. We are glad to hear that Dr. Weeks on hearing of Dr. Slayter's death manfully offered his assistance to the Government today. It is also gratifying to learn that only four deaths occurred last night, one on the island and the rest on board.

"Dr. Garvie in his report to the Provincial Secretary this morning says: 'I am glad to assure you that the disease on the hulk *Pyramus* is rapidly decreasing, as also on the shore, and that such is the improvement that with the cooperation of the medical officer of the ship and one passenger physician there is quite enough medical aid here. We are busily employed in making the people on shore as comfortable as possible, having the hulk cleared, and burying the dead.'"

In Halifax fear continued to rise. "A case of Cholera is reported from Point Pleasant today," came a *Citizen* report, "caused by the imprudent use of infected clothing washed ashore from the plague ship; and two other cases, it is said, have been discovered in Water Street. In spite of the utmost vigilance of the medical gentlemen in charge, considerable quantities of the wearing apparel and bedding of deceased persons instead of being burned or buried has been thrown into the tide and is now strewing the shores of the harbour. Several pieces of it have drifted into the docks and wharves of the city, and in the Dartmouth cove some of it has been dragged up on the beach by parties who were not aware of the risk they run. Under these circumstances nothing short of a miracle can prevent the spread of the contagion in the city. The steamer *England*, having been thoroughly fumigated, will leave for New York tomorrow with the convalescent crew and passengers."

Also on April 17, Dr. Garvie wrote to Tupper. " This evening's report of the state of the sick upon the steamer Hulk and shore is as follows," he transcribed tersely, "Island: Deaths 2, Sick 14, dying 2; Hulk: Deaths none, sick 7; Steamer All well."

Tupper responded to Dr. Garvie. "Sir," he wrote, "I have the honour to inform you that His Excellency the Lieutenant Governor has been pleased with the advice of his council to appoint you Health Officer of the Port of Halifax in place of the lamented Dr. Slayter. I have it in command from his Excellency the Lieutenant Governor to direct you to send the *England* away as soon as she is properly purified with all the passengers who are now well, as they will be much better situated than here and you will then be better able to manage those left under your care."

On April 17, 1866, as Dr. Slayter died of cholera on McNab's Island, Dr. Charles Tupper put forward a resolution for Canadian union in the Nova Scotia House of Assembly. Another politician, Adams George Archibald, and three of his followers seconded the motion, and though roundly opposed by the large majority of Nova Scotians, the motion was carried thirty-one votes to eighteen. One who voted for the resolution, though well aware of the popular disagreement, noted that his earlier objections "vanished like smoke" because of the clear need to "save us from annexation or from invasion."

Fear had been a useful tool. As an anti-Confederation editorial in the *Citizen* noted, "The Fenians made their appearance in Eastport, [Maine] and forthwith the Confederation resolution was tabled in our House of Assembly. A few days after, the resolution was carried and presto! the Fenians had evaporated and gone." Howe biographer J. Murray Beck put it this way: "The evidence seems conclusive that a resolution for union could not have been carried in 1867 but for the Fenians."

I returned my papers to my bag and stood. Then I pulled the rucksack over my shoulder and started walking up the road, thinking about the Fenian threat that pushed Nova Scotians toward Confederation. Like so many fears, the reality was distinctly different from the perception.

The first Fenian invasion of Canada came at the same time as the cholera to McNab's, in April of 1866. A group of 300 Irish radicals had assembled themselves in Maine villages, including Pembroke, Eastport, and Calais, spending their time in the coffee shops and local taverns, rallying themselves to action. Likely they sang popular Fenian songs. One favourite went like this:

We are the Fenian Brotherhood, skilled in the arts of war,
And we're going to fight for Ireland, the land we adore.
Many battles we have won, along with the boys in blue,
And we'll go and capture Canada, for we've nothing else to do.

It was possibly after one rousing chorus of this tune, and certainly after more than one round of drinks, that those Fenians in charge thought it a fortuitous time to invade. Unfortunately, they had no weapons with them and not much of a plan. And yet, this somehow seemed less important than the decision to do something. It was suggested by someone in the group, with a logic that could only be acceptable under the influence of alcohol, that it would be just fine if their weapons followed them into Canada later by boat.

And so a group of six Fenians ceremoniously marched themselves to the waterfront, where they commandeered a small boat and promptly rowed to Indian Island, New Brunswick. Once ashore, the group slipped into town where a few of them shimmied up a flagpole and removed the Customs House ensign. Emboldened by their daring deed, the group raced back to their boat and rowed to Eastport, where they immediately cabled news of this grand achievement to the newspapers in New York. By morning sympathetic Irish papers heralded the raid with the headline "Daring Feat! Capture of a British Flag!"

Of course, once the actual details of this "daring feat" became known, few could do more than snicker. Making this inept effort all the more embarrassing, the boat that was ultimately commandeered by the Fenians to provide arms was seized by the U.S. authorities who then, with the help of two British vessels, surrounded the would-be invaders still milling about at the local taverns.

This embarrassing defeat notwithstanding, one Fenian was so determined to show his mettle that he undertook his own single-handed invasion. Somehow, in the course of an afternoon, he acquired a U.S. military uniform and donned it. He then offered a rousing toast to his success at the village tavern and promptly started toward the bridge into Canada at St. Stephen, New Brunswick. Halfway across, he was stopped by a curious U.S. sentry. Unable to explain himself, the frustrated Fenian pulled out his pistol and levelled it. His eyes wide, he made some grand declaration about Irish nationalism and then fired. Now whether due to the nature of nineteenth-century pistols, or to the potency of the grain alcohol served at the local tavern, the fiery Fenian's shot missed, whereupon the now angry U.S. sentry gave chase to the rogue invader all the way back into town. After that, the remaining Fenians not already captured by the British and Americans dispersed themselves.

Still, the would-be invaders' failure in Maine would not deter them from another try. In June of 1866, a Fenian force of some 650 to 1,300 crossed the Niagara River not far from Buffalo, New York, in canal boats towed by two slow-moving steam tugs. Upon arrival in Canada, they entered the modest village of Fort Erie, declaring it captured for the Fenian cause. The invaders then cut the telegraph lines, tore up a stretch of railway, and – for good measure – set fire to a nearby bridge.

That afternoon, a New York newspaper reported, "Intelligence is received that 1,500 Fenians effected a river crossing and landed in Canada about half-past three o'clock this morning. The crossing took place at Pratt's Iron Furnace, and the landing was made at a point about a mile below Fort Erie. The ferriage was accomplished by means of two tugs with small canal boats, conveying about 1,500 men. About 200 men whom the boats could not accommodate were left on this side. They expect to follow shortly. The invaders were met with no interference or opposition. When they landed on the opposite shore, loud cheers were given which could be plainly heard on this side, together with the sound of drum and fife."

Some of the raiders wore buttons stamped with the letters IRA – Irish Republican Army – reportedly the first time such a designation was used. In any event, the Canadian militia responded the next day. In a disastrous engagement, nine militiamen were left dead and thirty-seven wounded. It would be considered the only Fenian victory. On the American side, U.S. forces arrived to prevent the additional crossing of Fenian soldiers, and soon the invaders in Canada found themselves cut off. Without support and supplies, they decided to return to Buffalo, where they promptly surrendered.

I considered the strange confluence of these events: Fenians, Confederation, and cholera; and the melding of fate and fear. The threads of my tapestry, it seemed, were cutting across each other, shaping each other, and changing each other.

Somberly, I also thought of Slayter's death. I imagined the messenger who arrived at Slayter's home, imagined the news he delivered to Slayter's wife with her children at her side. Fatefully, Slayter's was the last new case of cholera on the island. And I thought about how his fate was tangentially caught up with the fate of the Iranian bricklayer, the American missionary, the German and Irish emigrants, and the Fenian radicals. I wondered too if his fate was strangely caught up with that of Nova Scotia and Confederation.

I mused that a few days following the April 17 vote for Confederation, the *Citizen* ran the following obituary: "Died at Halifax, by a sudden stroke of Confederation, on the 17th April, Responsible Constitutional Government, a native of Nova Scotia, a lineal descendant of British Constitution Esq., aged 35 years. He died in the House in which he was born; his mortal remains will lie in State in the Council Chamber for three days, and will remain forever embalmed in the hearts of the people. His funeral obsequies will take place at Ottawa as soon as the Grand Trunk [Railway] is prepared to convey them. Messrs. Tupper, Henry, Archibald and McCully will remain at Ottawa to prevent a resurrection, the renegades will return to Arichat for absolution. His Excellency Sir F. Williams will leave his native land forever, and all who mourn his loss will wear crepe on their arm for 30 days."

The reaction to Confederation in towns and villages across Nova Scotia was equally noteworthy. The *Citizen* also recorded one telling event, with the headline "Excitement in Lunenburg. Two Men of Straw burned in Effigy." According to the paper, "A Bridgewater correspondent informs us by telegraph that great excitement has been caused there by the Confederation coup d'etat in the House. The effigies of Messrs. Jost and Kaulback [local politicians] were hanged and burned by the people – whose only regret seemed to be that the real 'men of straw' were not present in person."

Fear and fate, it seemed, somehow conspired to shape that dark day of April 17, 1866. And yet, as so often happens, wyrd's great tapestry had space for yet another thread – hope.

10

Contagion

"CONTAGION – The idea of contagion should be abandoned. All the missionaries who have been with the most malignant cases day after day are fully convinced of the non-contagiousness of the cholera. The incipient attacks which all have suffered from are to be attributed to great fatigue, making the constitution liable to attack."

– Dr. Cyrus Hamlin, Constantinople, 1865

As I reached the southern end of McNab's Pond, I was conscious that shadows now crisscrossed the path. Looking up, I saw patches of blue sky and, for a brief moment anyway, the sun peeking out amid the clouds. At the same time, I was also aware that the air was becoming increasingly humid. Since I was still wearing my rucksack and a light coat, I was beginning to feel uncomfortably warm.

I stopped in the road and removed my pack. From inside, I found a pair of khaki-coloured shorts and placed them on the ground. Then I rolled up my coat and tucked it inside the bag. Standing straight, I looked around for a place to change and, after a moment or so, realized, of course, that no such place was available. I smiled at my misplaced self-consciousness. After all, save for the odd, inebriated revolutionary, I was effectively alone on the island. So I ignored my flash of modesty and removed my pants. And for a moment, I stood there in the road, holding my jeans in my hand – wearing little more than my briefs and a smile – reflexively scanning the woods for voyeuristic wildlife and, somewhat tangentially, thinking about the Romanian reaction to the 1866 cholera epidemic.

Back then, as the cholera raged in central Europe, many of the locals turned to folk remedies and folk tales as a means to make sense of the catastrophic illness that had descended upon them. Among the Romanians, many villagers turned their attentions to a spirit named Dschuma. Dschuma was sometimes seen as a wailing virgin or an old witch. In either case, she was understood to be the physical embodiment of disease. It was said that Dschuma suffered interminably from the cold and was, thus, imagined as interminably naked. And so, in the way of folk wisdom, village maidens traditionally made garments to ward off Dschuma, hanging the clothes for her to take.

In any case, as the cholera raged through central Europe in the summer of 1866, there came news from a small village deep in the Wallachia district of Romania that a group of young maidens had removed their clothes and, using a ploughshare, dug a deep furrow around their entire village. As the nubile maidens later explained, they had done this as a blocking charm against Dschuma. History does not indicate whether their charm worked, but we can safely assume that the young village males thought the effort most worthy.

With my thoughts vaguely on Dschuma, and naked maidens plowing fields around Romanian villages, I rolled my jeans into a ball and tucked them into my rucksack. Then I put on my shorts. Feeling considerably cooler now, I pulled the ruck-sack back over my shoulder and started walking north again. As I did, the thoughts of the Romanian reactions to the cholera also got me thinking about the similarly strange English reactions to the epidemic.

On a bright Sunday morning on August 12, 1866, Reverend James Augustus Atkinson, Rector of Saint John's Longsight, England, educated at Eton and Exeter College, Cambridge, stepped to his pulpit to deliver his regular Sunday sermon. His topic for that day was certainly provocative. It was entitled "The Cholera: Is it the Visitation of God?" Whether he felt the cholera was indeed a supernatural visitation or was instead the result of something more scientific remains unclear. However, this need to publicly consider the question spoke powerfully to the irrational fear of those in England who, under threat of the epidemic, were not unlike the villagers of Romania in need of some supernatural explanation for what was, to them at any rate, unexplainable.

Atkinson was not alone. Also that summer, in 1866, the Reverend Charles Kingsley, Rector of the church in Eversley, asked his congregation a similar question. In his sermon, he accepted that "cholera comes by no miracle, but by natural causes." Yet he also noted, with a touch of divine determinism, that this "does not prevent its being a visitation of God." Indeed, he went on to argue, "[T]his minute an invisible cholera seed is the minister of God, by which he is visiting from house to house, searching out and punishing certain persons who have been guilty, knowingly or not, of the offence of dirt; of filthy and careless habits of living; and especially, as has long been known by well-informed men, of drinking poisoned water. Their sickness, their deaths are God's judgment on that act of theirs ... [T]oo many of the labouring classes in towns, though they are earning very high wages, are contented to live in a condition unfit for civilized men."

Still pondering these reactions to the epidemic, I again passed McNab's Pond, its brown muck seeming somewhat less noxious under the now partly blue sky. As I looked across the cove toward Hugonin Point, I imagined the anchored *Pyramus* and the S.S. *England*, which was now preparing to depart for New York.

On April 18, 1866, *The Halifax Citizen* reported the death of William Valentine, Esquire, Provisions Merchant of Dublin by "apoplexy, on board the National Steam Navigation Co's steamship *England*, Quarantine Station, Halifax, N.S." In a peculiar instance of class bias, the paper was careful to note that Valentine was a "saloon passenger to New York." Conversely, with great enthusiasm, the paper also reported that "as the yellow flag [over the S.S. *England*] was hauled down three heartfelt cheers were given."

As well, on April 18, 1866, Dr. Gossip wrote to Charles Tupper. "Sir," he began, "We are now taking all the healthy passengers from the island to the steamer and will be very busy all day. The reports this morning from the quarantine are very cheering. I would like to know from Mr. Morrow of [supplying] the sick who will be left behind after the departure of the *England*. A saloon passenger [walking last night] up on the quarterdeck was seized with apoplexy and fell on the main deck. He was taken up dead. I have no objection to Dr. Wickwire acting as assistant Health Officer. Some arrangements will have to be made to send us assistance after the departure of the *England* as the sick will have to be cared for and the dead buried and we will be left with few men from the shore as who have been cleaning the steamer and who, I am afraid, will object to do the work."

Tupper wrote back immediately. "Since writing my letter to you of this morning," he noted, "I have received yours of today and will make arrangements to meet your wishes respecting the case of the sick, food assistance, etc. Let me know at once how many will be left on the *Pyramus* and how many on shore and furnish a detailed report respecting the whole affair as soon as you can."

Henry Wenner recalled that "on the 18th, after the ship had been cleaned, we were again taken aboard." When the ship was fully boarded, a deeply relieved Captain Grace gave the orders at seven o'clock, and the S.S. *England* set sail for New York. As Reverend Martin remembered, "[B]y the energy and charity of the Board of Health officers our health certificate was signed in due form. The odious yellow flag came down and three hearty cheers of all on board. Our anchor is weighed, and we steam ahead slowly from the scene of misery, sickness and death with a joy still mingled with sorrow, for we leave twenty-four of our companions still sick on the island. Some two or three days bring us to an anchor in the Quarantine waters, Lower Bay, New York."

At Government Wharf, I again walked out to the end and took in the imagined scene. By the end of the day on April 18, the dire atmosphere of the day before had already begun to abate. On the island and in the city, there was a growing sense that the illness was finally receding. On the next day, April 19, 1866, the *Citizen* reported on the improved situation. "The latest tidings from the quarantine station convey the gratifying information that the plague is now diminishing rapidly, and in a few days will have ceased entirely."

The paper also related that "the [remains of the] late lamented Dr. Slayter who died so heroically at his post of duty were interred [on McNab's Island] at high twelve, with proper Masonic ceremonies by the officers, medical gentlemen and passengers of the steamer *England*, many of whom belong to the Fraternity. The funeral scene is said to have been sadly impressive. Peace to the ashes, and honour to the immortal memory of a noble physician and brave gentleman!"

Additionally, the paper reported, "Yesterday morning, an unfortunate cabin passenger fell from the berth in his stateroom in the vessel's poop[deck], and broke his neck. We could not learn his name." The *Citizen* also noted, "We regret that the statement has been made public that Patrick Reardon, cooper, fell overboard from the *England* in a state of intoxication, as we have positive information that such was not the case. He had bravely volunteered to help in attending the sick on board the *Pyramus* and died while discharging his duties. His remains were interred on the beach. His untimely end has caused great distress to his widowed mother and other relatives with whom we deeply sympathise."

With the departure of the S.S. *England*, optimism crept back into the city. "We learn that two deaths occurred yesterday," read the paper, "and that only sixty passengers are left on McNab's Island. There is not the slightest trace of the disease in the city or the suburbs, and sanitary regulations are now promptly enforced. It is said that two of the city police have resigned rather than do duty on board the guard ship near the quarantine station. They are better out of the force to which such cowardice could only bring disgrace if sheltered by the police uniform, and their names ought to be given to the public. The S.S. *England* sailed away for New York last evening with all the convalescent passengers. At a sanitary meeting in Richmond, Virginia, one of the doctors in Council said that the steamer *England* had passed through Cholera atmosphere, which was on its way across the Atlantic, and thus the passengers contracted the disease."

Early on April 19, Dr. Gossip reported to Charles Tupper. "Sir, The following is the report of cases on the Island at 5 p.m. 10 Sick; 30 Well; 1 Dead. Two who are out in tents this morning were not sent in last report. On board the *Pyramus* 2 Deaths; 5 Sick; 4 Well."

At ten o'clock he wrote again. "The steamship *England* sailed last night for New York taking on board all the healthy passengers (the sick and ailing being left behind on the island and in the *Pyramus*) with the exception of a few who preferred remaining to being separated from other members of the family.

"I received yours of yesterday but was unable to answer it as it was impossible to ascertain how many persons would be left on the island until the healthy passengers were all on board and the *England* sent to sea and by that time communication with the city had ceased for the day. I now send report at 10 o'clock a.m.: On board *Pyramus*: Sick – 4; Dead – 0; Well – 4 On Island: Sick – 12; Dead – 3; Well – 27 Leaving on island and in the hulk 50 persons. Besides these, we have a steward of the *England* who volunteered to stay, the storekeeper of the *Pyramus* and 19 from the city, who I am happy to state are quite well up to the present.

"There are still a number of bodies, some coffined, some not, on the island and the men here object to perform the rather disagreeable duty. I would wish if possible to have a party of men for that duty. I also wish to remove the tents from their present position and put them up in a better position and have the sick removed into them."

From the wharf, I looked back at the hill behind me and imagined the abandoned tent village. I watched as the city volunteers gathered clothes and bedding and placed the items into piles.

At midday of April 19, Gossip again wrote to Tupper. "Before leaving," he began, "I gave Captain Grace of the *England* a certificate that the ship had been thoroughly scraped, scrubbed, whitewashed and fumigated and that, when leaving this port, there were no cases of disease on board. By returns to the Captain, the *England* sailed with 875 steerage and 16 saloon passengers, 116 crew including master. A lot of bedding which was not allowed on board the *England* is still on the Island and will be burned as soon as I can get hands to do the work.

"I have neither news nor ink on the island, so that I have to make my report in pencil. After this I will be able to send reports regularly and I trust and believe that as far as the sanitary condition of the island and hulk concerned they will be satisfactory. Dr. Garvie and Mr. F. Garvie are at present on board the *Pyramus* and quite well. I beg to state that it is impossible or has been to reply to correspondence from the city without neglecting the sick."

That same afternoon, Tupper responded to Gossip. "Sir, I am directed by his Excellency, the Lieutenant Governor, to remind you that you had been sufficiently directed to communicate to me any aid that was required by you in the treatment of those under your charge, and to express the deep regret and astonishment upon learning that, without any communication to me that you required any supplies, you have seen proper to write to His Grace the Archbishop of Halifax 'We are positively in want of necessaries of life and comfort. We are in great need.' Mr. Morrow, upon whom has the duty of supplying everything required, informs me that he has promptly forwarded everything that has been sent for, that last night he received an order from you for bread and meat, which was forwarded, and that your requisition for other supplies was not received until afternoon today.

"It is not only painful but unjust to that gentleman that while engaged in immediately dispatching everything asked for, he should be assailed by rumours in the street of destitution and suffering, which, if it exists, can only be resulted from a failure on your part to ask earlier for what you required. I am farther directed to [impose] upon you the necessity of making timely application to Mr. Morrow or to the government for anything that is required ... and communicate to me any failure to obtain whatever you may require before adopting a course calculated to excite an impression that the government and [members of] the ship are not discharging their duty to these unfortunate strangers.

"Mr. Morrow informs me that he is making every effort to get parties to bury the dead but it is very desirable that no effort should be spared to induce the parties now on the island to discharge that duty and ... putting any larger number of persons than can be avoided in quarantine."

The next morning, on April 20, 1866, Gossip responded to Tupper. His letter notably makes no mention of Tupper's sharp rebuke, suggesting perhaps that Gossip was singularly interested in the well-being of the emigrants and the containment of the illness, protocol be damned.

"Sir," Gossip began, "I beg here to report from your information that although there are still some cases of sickness, mostly fever, on the island, no new cases of cholera have occurred for the last 48 hours. We are today busily engaged in burying the dead and trying to make this part of the island as healthy as possible. I append a report of the state of the island and *Pyramus* up to 7 p.m.

"The Sisters of Charity have been unremitting in their attentions to the children placed under their charge and the cheerful manner in which they have cooperated with the medical men demands our heartfelt acknowledgement, although the medical men here would be sorry to lose their services yet as the duties which they were sent here to perform are at an end. I would suggest that they might be allowed to return to the city after tomorrow. They have had no communication with the sick. Father McIsaac also wishes to return.

"Together with the military I have established regular quarantine bounds. A number of persons living out of bounds are out of provisions and have applied to me for permission to visit the city. I myself do not think there would be any danger, but I would wish to have some definite instructions about the matter. Are the police from the city under my orders and can I put them on duty on the island? I would wish you to send me officially a copy of the Port regulations and a statement of the duties required of me under the present circumstances. If

I could obtain the services of the Police and the specials ... I would dispense with the Military force ...

"We have among the sick several more cases of typhus ... the only way in which a report can be obtained of the state of the people on the island is by a personal visit through the huts, counting as you go. This is very subject to fallacy as I have counted them five or six times today and every time with a different result. On account of the difficulty of obtaining men to work here, I have been unable to get the people out of the woods, as I intended, but I hope to be more successful tomorrow when they shall be all mustered and properly classified."

Back in Halifax, the city council considered a proposal for the erection of a monument "to the memory of the lamented Dr. Slayter, who sacrificed his life to stay the plague in our harbour." The *Citizen* suggested that a "suitable style would be a grand obelisk of native granite paneled with marble; and it should be erected on some conspicuous point on McNab's Island, where the crews of every passing vessel might observe it and be reminded or informed of the heroism of him whose name will ennoble the stone on which it is graven. Thus the scene of his loss will become the site of his immortal honour, and no one will think of Halifax Harbour without remembering brave John Slayter.

"But the best monument after all, to his memory, and one which should precede the other, is a Fund for the education of the Doctor's young children. He, their natural protector and supporter, has died in the public service; and we trust therefore that our Legislature will make a liberal grant for an object which will meet the unanimous approval of the country."

It is unclear whether the city council agreed to fund this proposal, but the memorial was never constructed. In fact, save perhaps for the white crosses in the McNab family cemetery, I found no physical remains to evoke this dark tale. Looking across the cove to Hugonin Point, I thought of the victims still lying in the red clay of the Lawrencetown Till. Perhaps there, somewhere on the point, I would find a memorial or a marker or some tangible proof of these events. So I gathered my things, and retreated from Government Wharf, turning left as I reached Garrison Road.

On April 21, the *Citizen* reported, "The latest accounts from the quarantine station, furnish the agreeable news that the cholera is fast disappearing. Only some sixty persons are left there, the *England* having taken away about 890. There was one death yesterday among the few cases still left on the *Pyramus*.

"One of the medical attendants, Mr. Frank F. Garvie had a second attack of the disease on Thursday morning but soon recovered. We daresay the medical staff will not grumble much when the close of the quarantine brings their dangerous and arduous toils to a close. The Sisters of Charity and Roman Catholic Clergymen who have gone down to the station have also been assiduous and untiring in their efforts to tend the sick and dying, without distinction of creed. Rev. Mr. McIsaac, we are glad to learn, has recovered from his sickness.

"We regret to learn that Pilot No 16, James Terence, residing in Portuguese Cove died on Thursday night of disease contracted on board the S.S. *England*. He had previously lost two of his children, young girls, and [the] other two are dangerously ill. The bodies of the children were conveyed to the burial place on sleighs drawn by long ropes to prevent contact and contagion.

"The disease is also in the house of another man named Purcell, who was in the pilot boat, and his daughter who washed his clothes on his return is now dying of the disease. It is well to state that Rev. Mr. Carmody is judiciously and indefatigably exerting himself to prevent the spread of the contagion in the Cove, by a rigid system of isolation and other proper precautions. The Government sent down Dr. Pryor and a nurse, yesterday."

On the same day, Charles Tupper wrote to Dr. Gossip. "Sir," he began, "I am instructed to say in reply to your letter of yesterday that His Excellency, the Lieutenant Governor, is willing that the Sisters of Charity, who have not been in communication with the sick, should be permitted to remove to the Northwest Arm, provided they remain isolated for ten days subsequently, but that [it] is not considered advisable or prudent to permit the Rev. Father McIsaac to leave the quarantine station under existing circumstances.

"Any of the people on McNab's Island not having had communication with the quarantine station can visit the city with your written permission to enable them to pass to and fro. The Mayor is not willing that the police force should be made to do duty on the island and you had better therefore retain the military for that purpose.

"We are anxiously awaiting the detailed report as we are at present unable to give the information required in various quarters and which if not creditable to the medical officers that we should be without. I enclose a note from the mayor for your consideration. Do not hesitate to ask for tar of lime or anything required by the necessities for yourself and those around you to meet the [needs] of the care fully as otherwise the responsibility will rest upon you. I know of no Port regulations except the enclosed, of which you have been furnished with a supply. Your instructions as having charge of the quarantine station are simply to do everything that can be done to cure the sick and prevent the extension of the disease and you are clothed with absolute power for that purpose."

After passing most of McNab's Cove, I stepped off the path and made my way to the rocky beach that encircled Findlay's Cove. The rolling stones were just large enough to make walking difficult, and I stumbled along awkwardly. I stepped around bits of driftwood and green netting and ambled across a broad causeway with a large marshy area to my right and Findlay's Cove to my left. When the causeway ended, I climbed a steep knoll to my right, thick with tall grass and low bushes. The bushes were nearly leafless and repeatedly grabbed at my legs. After I had climbed a dozen yards or so, the ground levelled, and I came upon an old wooden fence, partly collapsed into a pile of sun-bleached wood. Behind this ran a rusted wire fence about chest high. It, too, had fallen into disrepair and a number of its posts now leaned low to the ground. Beyond this fence stretched a broad swath of tall grass and more scrub brush.

For a time, I searched the grounds with a hope of finding a marker or monument, but nothing obvious or hidden presented itself. So, finally, I walked closer to the cove side, remembering that those below in the cove could see the burial trench being dug. With nothing more to go on, I decided that this was the most likely spot. And so I sat and perused my notes.

On April 22, Gossip responded to Tupper. "I beg to report for your information the state of the quarantine station at McNab's Island. We have had no deaths for the last 24 hours and no new cases of sickness, though there are one or two dangerous cases on the island. I have appended a report from Dr. Garvie of the Hulk: I have the honour to report to you the hospital report, the Hulk *Pyramus* Sick – 5; Well – 4; Dead – 0. I have great pleasure in reporting to you that the state of the Hulk is so satisfactory ... I require no more medical assistance.

"I have attended to the burning of bedding on shore and have seen to the burning ... On [the] island [there are remaining] 45 persons; 13 [are] sick; 1 [is] dying; On [the] *Pyramus* 9 persons [remain]; 7 [are] sick; [there were] 2 deaths on shore; 3 [deaths] on [the] *Pyramus*.

"P.S. The stationery has been received but I have no ink or the bottles met with a mishap in coming from the *Pyramus* to the island. I have sent for more and as soon as it arrives I will be most happy to send my report in ink. Dr. Garvie, Mr. F. Garvie, and myself since our arrival at Quarantine have hardly had two hours of sleep a night. I will be asking Dr. Garvie to attend to the sick tomorrow and will answer as well as I can your communication of this evening. Gossip 7:30 p.m."

At ten o'clock the following morning, April 23, 1866, Dr. Gossip wrote a quick note to Tupper. "Sir," he wrote, "Again, I have the pleasure to report no deaths either on the Hulk or Island. Today I have the working party employed in carrying out the vacant tents and burning all the clothing and bedding belonging to the deceased passengers. All the dead have been interred."

Included in the note was Dr. Garvie's brief report. "I have the honour to report," wrote Garvie in a thin spidery hand, "that on board the Hulk *Pyramus* the report is the same as yesterday. I am now supervising the removal of all the passengers preparing to clean the hulk."

That same day, Dr. Tupper replied to Dr. Gossip. "I am instructed to call your attention to the necessity of great supervision to prevent any clothing bedding or other material being thrown into the sea from the island or *Pyramus*," wrote Tupper, "and to request you to prevent anything of the kind being done, as there is a good deal of alarm felt here. I will be glad if you will have all communications fumigated before being transmitted. Be good enough to furnish me with the best answer in your power at your earliest convenience with the means of replying to the letter from the Naval Authorities, of which you have a copy, and also a statement of the best treatment of the disease. The assistant health officer has been appointed for the purpose of discharging indispensable duties which could not be discharged by any person in quarantine but Dr. Weeks and several other medical gentlemen have placed their services at the service of the government who have hitherto not accepted them because they were from time to time informed by Drs. Slayter Garvie and yourself that no farther medical aid was requested. Yours faithfully, C. Tupper."

On Tuesday, April 24, 1866, the *Citizen* reported, "On Sunday last the Health Officer reported from the Quarantine

Station that no deaths had occurred since last report, and that all the corpses had been buried. The same encouraging report was received yesterday – but one death, an old case, took place last night.

"On Saturday the Sisters of Charity who had been so assiduous in tending the sick were relieved from their duties – and went from McNab's Island to the Northwest Arm, where they will likely remain a few days until all fear of carrying infection with them has passed. Drs. Garvie and Gossip, and Mr. Frank Garvie will remain on duty at the Quarantine Station during this week yet; and Rev. Father McIsaac also is still there. The health of the patients there is rapidly improving, and they will soon bear removal. Four barrels of chloride of lime were sent down on Sunday to be used for fumigating and cleansing the hospital hulk *Pyramus*. This process will be completed today.

"On Sunday a case of supposed Cholera, occurred in the old house in the southwest corner of the Bremner lot, at Freshwater bridge. The family in which it occurred, consisting of father, mother and two children, was removed to the City Hospital, and a policeman placed guard over the premises to prevent any person having access to the house. The building is old and of little value, and we believe will be destroyed by order of the Health officers. We were informed last evening that the child first attacked with the disease died in the hospital yesterday afternoon, and that the other child was dangerously ill.

"A meeting of the Board of Health was held yesterday forenoon when considerable discussion arose respecting the regulation of our Sanitary Affairs. The question of a suitable Quarantine Station was also discussed and a committee was appointed to confer with the Government on the advisability of purchasing Lawlor's Island for that purpose. Devil's Island was spoken of, but the want of accommodation for ships beside it was urged as an objection. We understand that there is a current opinion that the Quarantine Station ought to be farther removed. Some propose that it should be established at Sambro, while others would transfer it to Margaret's Bay."

Two days later the paper reported, "On Tuesday evening the encouraging news was received from the Quarantine Station on McNab's Island that the cholera had almost entirely disappeared, although some cases of typhoid and spotted fever still required the attention of the medical staff. One or two cholera patients on the hulk *Pyramus* would not, it was feared, recover, but their cases were complicated by other disorders, such as mortification of the limbs and such. There are in all about forty-three of the *England*'s passengers left at the station.

"Dr. Gossip, Health Officer, who had hitherto escaped sickness, was somewhat ill on Tuesday, but we are glad to announce the young doctor's recovery. Dr. Garvie and Mr. Frank F. Garvie remain well, though hard worked. The arduous labours through which the three medical gentlemen have passed would severely test the strongest constitution. Everything has been done, however, to promote the comfort and relieve the wants of the sick. Rev. Father McIsaac still remains unflinchingly at his post of exalted duty, and his devotion to that duty is worthy of the highest commendation.

"The efforts of the medical gentlemen in regulating the quarantine affairs are admirably aided by Mr. George W. Rider, Sergt. Callaghan, and the men on the Island; while special credit is due to the policemen who have kept guard in the police boat over a fortnight without being relieved. Sergt. McGrath is still in quarantine, but Nicholas Power, David Power, and John Storey have been most vigilant and prompt in their duties – especially at night. We make this special mention of these men because we consider that everyone who has aided at the risk of his life in keeping the plague within its brittle bounds, deserves the acknowledgements and the rewards of the public.

"Messrs. Cunard & Co. have, as a matter of course, managed the responsible duties devolving on them as agents for the *England* here with the utmost tact and promptitude. Besides the constant personal exertions of J.B. Morrow, Esq., the agents have sent their dispatch boat twice each day regularly, and sometimes thrice each day, since the cholera ship came. Their boatman, Mr. Wm. Power, goes dauntlessly in the face of every risk with medicines, stores, official correspondence, &c., as promptly and regularly as if he felt that his rowboat must in its own way, as well as the *Cuba*, uphold the credit of the Cunard Line. Supplies have also been promptly forwarded by the special contractor Mr. J.E. Keating.

"As there have been many complaints respecting the bedding and clothing thrown from the infected ship into the harbour, it is well to state that this was done by those on board the *England* when she arrived. Dr. Slayter on discovering the practice, stopped it by the most stringent orders, and the utmost care was taken by him and the other doctors to recover and destroy all the bedding, blankets, &c. they found in the water within reach. The men on the police boat have also been on the look out for those floating articles, and have destroyed them whenever found.

"We understand that the police on the Island have discovered a man who allowed himself, for a large sum of money, to commit the grave offence of conveying to the Eastern shore the five passengers who escaped from the *England*. He has been arrested. We learn that notice was sent to Mr. Morrow today that passengers at the Quarantine Station are so far recovered and healthy that he can send for a vessel to convey them to New York as soon as he likes."

As I sat quietly on the grass of Hugonin Point, and the sun now shone steadily in the partly cloudy sky, I looked out over McNab's Cove and at the water now a dark blue. Despite my long day's search, I had found no physical remains of the horrific events of April 1866. Beneath me, perhaps, below the long yellow grass and broken-down fences, were the bones of the cholera victims now enveloped by the rich, red clay of the Lawrencetown Till. I mused that the history of the island presented itself in layers, the deep till reaching back tens of thousands of years; then, above it, the ancient human middens, reaching back thousands of years; and above that, reaching back more than a hundred or so years, the bones of cholera victims; and above these still, myself and my search for haunting memory whispers in the wind. The strands of my story had come together, pulled and tugged, and then spread apart, each carrying forward a part of the story, which, in turn, would affect all stories that followed.

With these thoughts filling my mind, I stood and began my descent from Hugonin Point. One final time, I passed McNab's Cove, then continued along Garrison Road, until I turned down Wreck Cove where I was to meet Captain Red Beard. Along the way, I continued to ponder the threads of wyrd's tapestry.

Conclusion

"'Tis fine for us to speculate and elect our course, if we must accept an irresistible dictation."
– Ralph Waldo Emerson, Concord, 1860

*I*n 1865, while still attending to the sick and dying in Constantinople, Dr. Cyrus Hamlin happened upon an old Turk in the streets who was eating a cucumber purchased from a nearby market. Hamlin was concerned that the cucumber carried cholera, so he warned the old man to throw away his meal. The old man just looked at Hamlin and smiled. "If I was born to die of cholera," he said, "I will die of cholera when the time comes, no matter what I eat or where I eat it." According to Hamlin, the old man died of cholera that evening.

I thought for a time about fate and fear as I wandered about the beach at Wreck Cove, waiting for Captain Red Beard to return. The water in the cove was now calm, reflecting a light blue. I kicked at stones in the damp sand along the water's edge and then wandered to the top of the beach, where I sat on a long sun-bleached board that looked as if it had once been part of a wharf. There, I read the final newspaper clippings and reports.

Through late April and early May, 1866, the *Citizen* reported that "John McPherson, second son of David McPherson, [had died] in the 19th year of his age." His funeral was set for the following afternoon "at 3 o'clock from his late residence, 80 Gerrish Street. Friends and acquaintances are respectfully requested to attend without farther notice." Also having died, Elizabeth Yeasie, "in the 46th year of her age, after a short but severe illness, which she bore with Christian resignation ... she has left a husband and 4 children to mourn her irreparable loss." Her funeral would take place at "her late residence, No. 21 Creighton Street" the next day "at 4 o'clock." Dying in her "81st year" was Mrs. Sarah Hoyne, a native of Kilkenny, Ireland. Her funeral would be held "from her daughter's residence near Canal Bridge on Monday next at 3 o'clock. Friends and acquaintances are requested to attend without farther notice."

In the local courts, John Percy was charged with being drunk but excused. Michael Drew was also found to be drunk and "fined $1." John Smith, drunk and disorderly, was "fined $4." Thomas Woodling, having been arrested for "annoying persons," had his case dismissed. Eliza Smith, however, for "making use of profane language," was given "30 days." William Miller, "drunk and crying murder" was "fined $2." Morris Lawson, William Dooly, and Michael Conners were all charged with being drunk. Morris was excused, while William and Micheal were fined "$2" and "$3" respectively. Seaman William Barley of H.M.S. *Tamar* was also charged with being drunk and "sent on board" his ship. Margaret Schofield, an old offender," was given "30 days" in prison. Charles Grant was "sentenced to keep the peace towards his wife for 12 months, for assaulting her." Fined $20 was "John O'Brien, for having his tavern open on Sunday." And "John Cody, for violating the ordinance respecting cabs, [was] fined $1."

Elsewhere, "The American Counsel paid an official visit to the U.S. warships in harbour to-day, and was saluted in due form by the *Augusta*." Also in the city, the newspaper reported, "Rails are being laid connecting Cunard's wharf with the street railway, so as to permit the freight cars to be loaded with merchandize from the steamers. The large car depot at Richmond is also nearly finished."

In Kings County, reported a headline in the *Citizen*, "The Action of the Legislature Unanimously Condemned." At the same time in Kentville, "At the Mass Meeting held here to-day, about fifteen hundred persons were present from all parts of the County. Mr. Howe spoke for two hours and a half, and was followed by Messrs. Moore, Brown, Weatherbee, DeWolf, Troop, Garvie, and Weeks, all opposed to Confederation. Messrs. Bill and Hamilton were called upon to resign their seats. Messrs. Moore and Brown were thanked for their action in the Assembly. Prominent Conservatives and Liberals alike moved and seconded resolutions of the same nature as those passed at the Hants meeting. All passed unanimously."

Also in the city of Halifax, "A little boy about three years old, dressed in blue jacket and pants, and wearing a black Kossuth hat, strayed from home this morning, and cannot since be found. Anyone seeing or hearing anything of him would oblige his parents by leaving word at the office of the *Evening Express*, Bedford Row. Another 'stray' little girl of between three or four years is also missing from her home. For particulars see advertisement." The advertisement appeared at the bottom of the page in small block letters. "Advertisement," it read, "Child Lost. Strayed from No. 100 Cunard Street, North side of Common, a little girl between three and four years old; brown frock, checked pinafore, black straw hat. Answers to the name of Sophia Jean. Any information respecting her will be thankfully received by her parents, at the above address."

In the shipping news, the paper reported that "on Thursday night last, the R.M.S. *Africa*, when entering the harbour, ran into and sank a small schooner supposed to be the *Good Intent*, bound from this port to Mahone Bay. This accident occurred somewhere off Sambro, and all on board the schooner were unfortunately drowned. The number of persons lost is uncertain, and is variously stated at from two to five."

In the city, the possibility of infected clothing and bedding floating to shore caused great concern. The rumours about how the clothing and bedding were handled caused boatman William Powers to offer a letter of correction to *The Halifax Citizen* on Saturday, April 28, 1866, under the headline "The Truth About the Infected Bedding Stories."

"Dear Sir," he began. "As there has been a great deal said lately about the bedding and clothing and so forth, floating from the hospital ship *Pyramus*, I would like to set the public mind at rest on the subject. I have been communicating with the steamship *England* twice and thrice a day regularly since her arrival amongst us, and also with the quarantine station from eight in the morning until late at night, when the water was rough and smooth. I consider that no one has had a better opportunity of seeing the infected clothing, bedding, or otherwise, floating from the S.S. *England*.

"Since the appointment of Dr. Gossip as Health Officer, I have never seen any clothing or bedding floating between the Police boat and the *Pyramus*, but I have seen a good many old beds and so forth thrown from Merchant vessels on arriving in the harbour, which has been done years before the *England* came in our midst, as every honest fisherman that attends the market can certify, a circumstance that would be unnoticeable at any other time. We must therefore expect to see some clothing washed ashore for some time to come, when it blows hard from the south and southeast, especially on McNab's Island, George's Island and Point Pleasant.

"I have made this statement merely because I have heard several people talk that know nothing at all of the matter. William Power, Boatman to Messrs. Cunard and Co."

I also read of Dr. Tupper's one direct experience with the cholera, a tale he related in a letter.

"One Sunday morning [April 29, 1866]," Tupper recalled, "a poor man, living in a small isolated house near the shore on the outskirts of Halifax, asked me to visit his child. The moment I saw the little girl it was evident that it was the dread disease. I called a policeman and told him not to allow anyone to enter or leave the house until I returned, then drove straight to the hospital, where I arranged for a room to be completely isolated. I then took the horse out of my wagon and put it in the ambulance, drove back to the house, took the sick child, with her father and mother, into the ambulance, and placed them in the isolated part of the hospital.

"As soon as I saw the child I asked the mother if she had used anything that had washed ashore from the ship *England*, which was anchored about a mile distant. She said she had not. The child and mother died, and the father, who was attacked, recovered. The mother before her death confessed that she found a piece of fine canvas on the shore, and made a petticoat for the little girl. I had the house and all it contained burned the next day. No other case occurred in Halifax. No more conclusive evidence has ever been given of the contagiousness of Asiatic cholera."

On April 30, Charles Tupper and the city health officials lifted the quarantine on McNab's. "The Quarantine term on McNab's Island has now expired," read the *Citizen*, "and free access to and from it is now permitted. The Policemen have been relieved from their grand boat duties, and returned to town this afternoon. The Medical staff still remains at the Station, however, in charge of the remnant of the *England*'s passengers, until these are taken to New York." While I read about the quarantine being lifted, I heard the whine of Captain Red Beard's boat cutting across the channel from Lawlor's Island.

Watching the boat move toward the shore, I let my mind return to the last of the quarantined emigrants.

"The remnant of the *England*'s passengers," noted the paper on April 28, "left at the Quarantine Station, McNab's Island, embarked on board the steamer *Louisa Moore* last evening. Before they went on board the emigrants, especially the women, were presented with clothing, and small sums of money, the proceeds of the charitable subscription fund started so generously in this city lately. The steamer sailed for New York this morning."

On May 1, and for the next two days, the citizens of Halifax watched great fires burning through the night on McNab's Island where "all the fragments and debris of the infected clothing still left at the station" were set ablaze.

Reported the *Citizen*, "We learned on Saturday that the crew of the S.S. *England* who undertook the burial of the bodies of those who died at first in the harbour of cholera, in the sands at Thrum Cap performed their work so inefficiently that the corpses became last week exposed to view – forming not merely a ghastly spectacle, but a horrible source of fresh contagion and pestilence. To prevent such a calamity, Mr. Frank Garvie went from the Quarantine Station with a burial party on Saturday and attended to the dangerous but necessary task of properly covering up the dead – about eighty in number – in permanent graves.

"We notice in the New York papers that there was one death on board the S.S. *England* on her voyage hence to New York, but the case was that of a child with whooping cough; and not the slightest trace of cholera could be found on her arrival, so thorough had been the sanitary operations of our Halifax medical staff."

In New York City, the *Times* reported, "At a recent meeting of the New York Board of Health a Dr. Parker reported a case of Asiatic cholera at Haverstraw; and introduced certain sanitary resolutions, providing for the removal of the cellar populations of New York and Brooklyn to more healthful quarters, for extra hospital accommodations and the appointment of physicians conversant with cholera treatment to useful positions. It was also suggested that the use of veal and other young meats be interdicted.

"In offering these resolutions the doctor said: 'Two ships have lately arrived in this country with cholera on board – the *England* of Halifax, and the *Virginia* at our own port – both crowded with emigrants. It is also said that the emigrants on board the Virginia were in a state of perfect health when starting on their voyage, and before leaving their own countries. For seven days of the voyage no sickness appeared among them; but on the eighth day the cholera broke out on board.

"'My conviction is, if it be true that the passengers were all in good health when they embarked that this disease was bred among them. Now in relation to the place in the ship where the epidemic first made its appearance: did it break out in the upper deck, in the cabin, or the lower decks? No. But where the air was stagnant and foul, where darkness prevailed, down in the depths of the hold. I understand that the disease made its appearance in the same manner on the *Atlanta*. She and *Virginia* have double tiers for the accommodation of the emigrants, and in both cases the cholera broke out in the lower tier, just where I would suppose it would.

"'It is futile for us to take measures for the prevention of the disease if we do not look round about us for the relief of those who live in those filthy cellars in certain parts of the city.'"

When Captain Red Beard's boat finally arrived at the beach, the captain deftly repeated his movements of the morning, jumping into the water and pulling the bow of the aluminum skiff onto the shore. I stood and walked over to greet him. He asked if had had enjoyed myself. I nodded and said that I had. And while the good captain held the bow, I climbed clumsily into the boat. Then, after pushing the skiff back into the water, the captain climbed aboard, started the engine, and turned the bow back toward Fisherman's Cove.

On May 8, *The Halifax Citizen* published the results of a city committee struck to provide a set of precautions in the event of another epidemic. Their conclusions perpetuated the same truths and myths of Cyrus Hamlin's letter. "The committee of the Medical Society," began the report, "appointed some time ago to prepare a code of rules for the guidance of the citizens in the case of a visitation of cholera, or for warding off attacks of that disease, have reported the following which have been approved by the City Medical Officer, adopted by the City Council, and are now published for general information:

"1st – Do not become alarmed. Persons in vigorous health have little or nothing to fear from contagion. Fear is a predisposing cause of the disease.

"2nd – Give prompt and early attention to any looseness of the bowels or diarrhea by lying down immediately, and sending for medical advice. Looseness of the bowels is the beginning of the disease.

"3rd – Use freely chloride of lime in your houses, cellars, yards, and in every place that is foul, by wetting it and distributing the article about the premises in plates.

"4th – Live temperately. Avoid the use of alcoholic drinks entirely. Keep good hours, avoiding the night air and the early morning dews, as well as crowded assemblies.

"5th – Keep the body clean, and the mind free from all excitement.

"6th – Give notice early of any sickness in your family, that immediate attention may be given to it by your physicians, or by the proper authorities.

"7th – Whitewash your cellars, shops, alleys, fences, and keep your houses clean and well aired.

"8th – Avoid eating unripe fruit or other indigestible food, and everything else that will in any way tend to produce looseness in the bowels.

"9th – Do not keep any dead animal, or decayed meats, or stale oysters, or spoiled potatoes, or either decayed vegetables, about your premises. Have them removed at once, covered with chloride of lime, or buried.

"10th – At the commencement of the disease wrap warm flannels around the body, and put the feet into a mustard bath. If vomiting be severe apply a mustard poultice to the pit of the stomach.

"11th – Wear flannel next to the skin, and at all times maintain the natural temperature of the body by a sufficient amount of clothing. Avoid exposure to sudden changes of temperature, and if accidentally caught in a storm, remove wet boots and clothing as soon as possible."

Reaching Fisherman's Cove, I offered Captain Red Beard my thanks and climbed onto the wharf. I looked one final time at the north end of McNab's Island and then turned away, wandering back through the tourist cottages and then to the parking lot, which now boasted ten or fifteen cars. There, tired and hungry, I tossed my bag into the backseat of my car. Turning the key, I started the engine. Then I pulled out of the parking lot and headed back to the city.

In the same newspaper and on the same day as the cholera committee report, there appeared this advertisement: "DR. BELL wishes to let his friends know that he has returned from the United States, and has resumed his practice at his old stand, No. 1 Maitland Street. He has had great experiences in the Cholera at Gibraltar, and other places, and he can solemnly say he never lost a patient he administered to in that disease, and which was not a few; and every one who wishes to try his

Medicine for the Cholera and all inward diseases would get immediate relief.

"He would announce to his friends that he has received a large stock of the purest medicines by the latest arrivals from England and France. He still recommends his celebrated Tonic Medicines, for different diseases as follows: His Bloodroot Pills and Medicine for Dropsy; his Hrysipelas Pills and Ointment, and his Pill Ointment, which gives immediate relief in the worst of cases; his Sarsaparilla, Burdock, and Root Bitters will be found a most excellent remedy for Liver Complaint and all Skin Diseases, and particularly beneficial to those who are of Costive or Dyspeptic habits.

"His Ointment for long-standing Sores will be found most excellent for healing. He can highly recommend his Cough and Phthysis mixture. He has found out a most excellent remedy for King's Evil, for Glandular Swellings, or any Eruptions, that will give immediate relief. His medicines for Tape Worms and other Worms will be found very good. His applications for Rheumatism and Lumbago will be found most excellent, as it is used inward and outward; they give relief very soon. He has been very fortunate in removing a great many Tumors and Cancers lately without cutting, and still recommends those who are troubled with that disease to come in time, which makes the cure very easy both for himself and for the patient."

As I drove across the Macdonald Bridge, I thought about the confluence of story threads, about how the actions of all participants created a grand tapestry of time and tale. And I thought about how these threads still continued forward. In the end, nearly four hundred of the thirteen hundred passengers had died, as well as many of the volunteers. Yet the many individual threads of those emigrants' lives had continued on. Though, in a sense, they simply disappeared into time's tapestry. The last piece of evidence of their existence was a single letter. On July 22, 1866, a group of surviving passengers from the S.S. *England* published in *The New York Times* a letter of thanks.

"To Captain Grace, NSN Company," the letter began. "Dear Sir, We the passengers on board the *England*, sailing from Liverpool to New York, cannot think of leaving the ship without tendering our grateful thanks to you and the officers under your command for the kind and courteous treatment we have received at your hands. We beg to say that the ship in every department, as far as we could see, is the very model of an emigrant ship for cleanliness and comfort. The gentlemanly demeanor, courtesy and attention to our wants, exhibited by you and your officers, are the most efficient means of securing to yourself and the company in whose service you are so usefully employed, the esteem and gratitude of the people.

"While we cannot take exception to any of the officers, we must in particular express our heartfelt thanks to the Medical Officer for his constant attention and courtesy to all....

"Neither should we forget your great kindness in allowing the brothers Nelson to entertain the passengers every evening by their extraordinary feats in acrobats and music (vocal and instrumental.) That you will long continue to serve not only the N.S. Company, but also the thousands of emigrants who may have the happiness of hereafter crossing the Atlantic under your care, is the prayer of your most obedient servants. The passengers."

And that, it seemed, was the end of my threads. My story was complete.

Still, some months later, as a light snow fell on a pleasant Sunday, I found myself walking along Robie Street in Halifax. Already my trip to the island seemed something of a dream, as did my story of a death ship in Halifax Harbour. But I was still troubled by having found nothing tangible from the past with which to connect my tale to the present. And as such, my story somehow felt incomplete. So, that Sunday, I set out for the Camp Hill cemetery, located just west of Citadel Hill, with the vague hope of finding the gravesite of Dr. John Slayter, who, after being buried on McNab's Island, was disinterred and buried there.

Opened in 1844 as a city cemetery, Camp Hill was and is large, divided into four quarters, with a gravelled road that runs around the outer edge and through the middle. Among its late luminaries are William Henry and Jonathan McCully, politicians who had helped Charles Tupper bring about Confederation. So, too, it was the final resting place of Joseph Howe, the anti-Fenian, anti-Confederation politician and newspaperman. As well, the cemetery held the bones of Abraham Gesner, who invented kerosene used in that old Martello Tower Lighthouse on Mauger's Beach. And, of course, it remains the final resting place of Dr. John Slayter.

After passing through the iron gates of the cemetery from Robie Street, I stopped and stared at the stone markers with little to direct me save for one cryptic mention in an 1892 article from *The Halifax Herald*. "This monument stands in the north western corner of the cemetery." Having entered from west side of the cemetery, I walked across the gravelled road and turned north onto the snow-covered grass by the first row of graves. By rough estimate, I figured this quarter of the cemetery represented a small city block, and so with a deep breath, and some well-placed optimism, I started up the first row.

I walked along the uneven ground, reading stone after stone. As I did, I gathered a cross-section of Halifax lives, my mind skipping from one age to another – from the late Victorian Age to World War One to the Cold War and back again – and imagining each life's story. At the end of the row, I turned sharply to the right, and ambled down another. After five or six rows, I stopped and began to wonder about my chances of success. The lettering on many of the stones – the older white granite ones, characteristic of the late Victorian period, and the period for which I was searching – had been badly weathered, and I wondered if I had already passed John Slayer's final resting place. Still, I continued on my search, up one row and down another.

Finally, having walked the length of the last row, I reached the gravelled path that divided the cemetery. But I had found no marker for John Slayter. So, I returned to the task and reentered the northwest section again, methodically retracing my steps, moving faster perhaps, but still scanning each stone for a familiar name.

Yet, when I reached my point of entrance again, with nothing to show for it except a chill, I knew that John Slayter's monument had either been too badly weathered or had crumbled and been removed. In either event, I had little choice but to accept fate. So I adjusted my collar, turned away from the stones and the cemetery, and headed back out onto Robie Street.

As I walked north, I gave one final thought to John Slayter's memorial. According to the *Herald*, the following words had been inscribed when the stone was placed in 1866: "This Memorial is erected by the Mayor and Alderman to mark the estimation entertained by the citizens for the heroic conduct of John Slayter M.D. late health officer for this port, who while in the discharge of his duty on board the steamship *England* in quarantine on the harbour of Halifax fell a victim to cholera April 17th 1866 in the 36th year of his age." How strange, I thought, that even carved into granite, the words had ultimately faded with time.

Yet, perhaps this was appropriate. Though I had found no tangible remains of the death ship in Halifax Harbour, I had found myself deeply entwined in its tapestry, the threads of which were woven into the fabric of the present day. After all, didn't the Fenian threat carry forward into the fight for Irish freedom? Didn't Charles Tupper's Confederation become the

Canada of today? And yet of the death ship and its people, I was somehow less certain. I still wondered: what, if any, meaningful thread was carried forward?

Then, as I watched the snow gently fall over the broad, open space of the Halifax Commons, it occurred to me that the singular, determined, human response to fear and fate in my tale had been hope, which is to say, paradoxically, ethereal hope was the death ship's most tangible thread.

And that, in the end, was enough for me.